A Book by
Donesa Walker

Written by: Donesa Walker
Design by: Will Baten

Dedication

After every storm in life there is a rainbow. Sometimes we have to search for it, sometimes we don't see it and sometimes it is a wonderful, immediate view. I am blessed with many rainbows that I see daily. These are the people in my life who spread sunshine through the storms, reflecting God's love despite their circumstances. I am so blessed to know them, write about them and love them.

My family both near/dear and far – you are rainbows in life to me. Some of you, like my precious brother Micah, I will only see on the other side in Heaven, but to the rest – thank you for reflecting the love of God daily.

To my wonderful editor and spouse – Wes; there are no words...thank you for 26 years of growth. You are the light of my life, sparkling through the rainstorms.

Table of Contents

Rainbow of the Soul

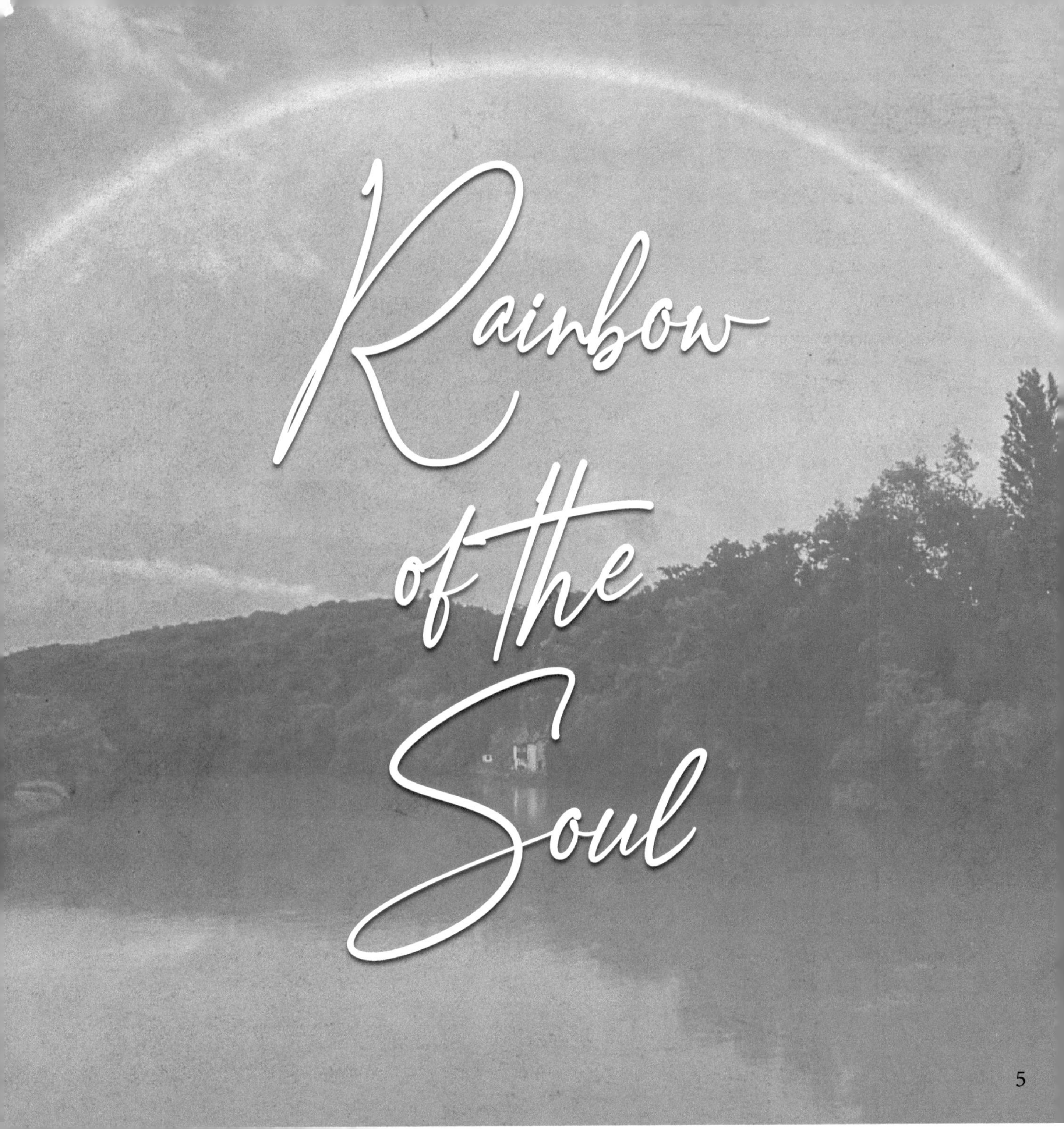

Grow a wise heart–you'll do yourself a favor;
keep a clear head–you'll find a good life.

Smart people know how to hold their
tongue;
their grandeur is to forgive and forget.

Mercy to the needy is a loan to God,
and God pays back those loans in full.

Fear-of-God is life itself,
a full life, and serene–no nasty surprises.
Proverbs 19: 8, 11, 17, 23

Life of Grandeur!

Forgiveness is where the wealth is at, as it is an investment that pays huge dividends! Wise hearts are those that lead to a clear head and smart people know how to choose their words wisely and mercifully. Respect for God, also known as fear of God, is the price of a serene life. Mercy given to others in the way of forgiveness is a loan that God pays back. When Wes and I first married we often fussed...well, that hasn't really changed a lot because we are both the eldest and think we are right a lot, but those early fusses were about winning – and holding our tongues was not a trait either of us had learned.

Needless to say...someone always had to have the last word (sorry, Wes)! Keeping a clear head was hard and emotions ran high and sharing everything was what you did...until we learned. The wise heart was birthed by learning to do ourselves a favor and leave the mud outside the house, both literally and figuratively. A clear head can listen with an open heart and not let emotional baggage cloud the judgement. Forgiveness was often, but forgetfulness wasn't so often; the mud of a previous disagreement got brought back into the house as a nasty surprise like doggy poo on the shoe. Many years of learning to forgive and realizing that God not only forgives – but also forgets – taught us that mercy is a loan that God pays back. Face it; people mess up. They mess up badly and often. Some of us are more prone to stepping in poo as we don't watch where we walk as carefully as we should. We tend to over-step into places we shouldn't or try to hop the fence into someone's business and instead we end up with mud (or worse!) brought into our relationships and we end up spreading that muck throughout the house. Relationships which take a lot longer to clean up often get ground into the carpet fibers, causing an incredible mess that takes years to clean. All of us desire a clean life, a life without nasty surprises and full of grandeur.

Forgiveness is the key to that. We must be willing to get down on our knees and clean the poo and ground-in mud from the carpets of our relationships through forgiveness and forgetfulness. If you keep on going back to the muck and bringing it back inside the house or relationship, you'll never have a life of grandeur, but rather one that has a constant need of cleaning - which is constant, dirty work. The key to a life of grandeur is forgetting what you forgave! Holding onto it is like holding onto the poo you have cleaned up off the floor until you decide to mess up your relationships/house again. So do yourself a favor - grow a wise heart. Forgive and then forget!

"I am the Good Shepherd. The Good Shepherd puts the sheep before himself, sacrifices himself if necessary. A hired man is not a real shepherd. The sheep mean nothing to him.
He sees a wolf come and runs for it, leaving the sheep to be ravaged and scattered by the wolf. He's only in it for the money. The sheep don't matter to him.
John 10:11-13

Sheeple!

Getting my mind set on God means that I focus on Him, not allowing other things to distract me; but the truth is – while that is how He feels about us – I'm not sure we are the same. You see, we are His sheep. I know that has negative connotations in society today but why is that? Sheep are perceived to be stupid animals who follow blindly when in fact they are not. While they are visual creatures due to their incredible peripheral vision which is twice that of humans, sheep are much like us. They have incredible memories and form lasting bonds with one another. They vocalize in different tones to speak; but honestly, while I think they are cute and beneficial, I don't have any connections with them other than scripture comparisons. Why? In Biblical times, sheep were a mainstay in the society. Jesus used the illustrations of sheep because people understood sheep and shepherding as a part of their everyday existence.

While I am not one to change God's word...here's my question: Who are your sheep? I own a small business and I can read this from that perspective because it speaks Jesus' intentions clearly. I am the Owner. The owner puts the clients before herself, sacrificing herself if necessary. The employee/trainer is not the owner; the clients do not mean as much to them. They see an alternate competitor coming and may choose to go work for them leaving the clients to be unattended and going to other businesses. The employee is there for a job and to get paid so the clients are not as important to them. I will say this is untrue for my business, but it works for a perspective.

The point is that you could read this as a parent and understand it too. I am a parent. A parent puts their child before themselves, sacrificing themselves if necessary. A babysitter isn't the child's parent. The children do not mean as much to them. They see an inappropriate television show and think nothing of letting the child watch it, never thinking that it could harm the child permanently and irrevocably. They are there for a job to get paid and the ultimate outcome doesn't affect them. I hope you are catching the drift – God (Jesus) is The Good Shepherd, The Business Owner, and The Ultimate Father. No matter what you perceive your sheep to be -from your kids to your livelihood – He's telling us that He cares far more for us than anyone else. Our government doesn't care for us. Our politicians don't care for us. Our society doesn't care for us. Our God does. We are His sheeple. We are the sheep/people of His pasture and He watches over us, cares for us, knows us and protects us with His own life.

Jesus asked the question of His disciples, "Do You love me?" When they answered affirmatively, He responded "Feed my sheep". So God's sheeple, whom are you feeding today?

God, you smiled on your good earth! You brought good times back to Jacob! You lifted the cloud of guilt from Your people, You put their sins far out of sight. You took back your sin-provoked threats, You cooled your hot, righteous anger. Love and Truth meet in the street, right Living and Whole Living embrace and kiss! Truth sprouts green from the ground, Right Living pours down from the skies! Oh yes! God gives Goodness and Beauty; our land responds with Bounty and Blessing. Right Living strides out before Him, and clears a path for His passage. Psalms85:1-3, 10-13

Right Living!

David celebrates in these verses, but in verses 4-9 he is pleading with God. Truth and right living are not always easy to swallow. Sometimes we don't want to hear the truth or accept it. It is much easier to put our heads in the sand and ignore what is in front of us than to embrace truth but love embraces truth just as right living embraces wholeness. We are so used to the I that we often fail to look at the reality. A coat of paint can cover mold but it won't kill it nor will it stay covered.

I watched a fascinating show on fungi and how they surround our lives - living beneath us, around us and IN us! They are vitally important to our survival, yet are rarely acknowledged. I thought…this is exactly as God is often neglected….He has created a fascinating world filled with intricacies we don't even understand and yet we try to lord our abilities away from Him. He must smile in humor at our naivety. As a parent who looks indulgently and mercifully on a child, God has constantly removed the clouds of guilt and stayed His wrath of judgment, but the Truth must meet with Love and embrace for Whole Living.

Accountability and willingness to brace hard truths about who we are, what we are doing and letting God reign over our hearts must be grasped for clear passage. I was recently told a truth about myself that I did not like. It hurt. It stung. I immediately pulled back from that person and that truth because they caused pain. It's hard to embrace truth sometimes when it has thorns, but this is the way to growth, happiness, love and whole living. Right living allows God's beauty and goodness to pour down upon us so that Truth sprouts and grows green from the ground.

Bounty and Blessings only come when you are willing to embrace the hard truths in love. Sometimes the truth delivered in love hurts and is hard to embrace but by doing so, you gain that merciful indulgent smile from a gracious God who showers you with His grace and goodness. Speak the truth in love. Embrace Truth with Love. This is the path to Right living!

Meanwhile, friends, wait patiently for the Master's Arrival. You see farmers do this all the time, waiting for their valuable crops to mature, patiently letting the rain do its slow but sure work. Be patient like that. Stay steady and strong. The Master could arrive at any time. Friends, don't complain about each other.

A far greater complaint could be lodged against you, you know. The Judge is standing just around the corner. Take the old prophets as your mentors. They put up with anything, went through everything, and never once quit, all the time honoring God.

What a gift life is to those who stay the course! You've heard, of course, of Job's staying power, and you know how God brought it all together for him at the end. That's because God cares, cares right down to the last detail.
James 5:7-11

Meanwhile, in the meantime...

Patience, my dear friends, is the toughest trait to train. It requires faith, hope, love, self-control and many times sheer grit. The gift of staying the course is full of rewards for those who never quit honoring God no matter what is done to them. This passage in James talks about the prophets of old, but let me tell you of the servants of today: I can see my parents and so many others who gracefully and fully walk this truth. God is taking many of them home as He begins to test the metal of this generation. Metal must be tested for weaknesses before it can be used especially in anything important because it cannot fail in time of need. I mean, who wants the metal on the airplane to fail as you are sitting in it thousands of feet up in the air?

In the meantime...a phrase that indicates a waiting place...is a place of forbearance and patience. It is the place of maturity and waiting, patiently allowing God's work to be fulfilled in you and perhaps never understanding the "why?" in the process. I don't understand why my brother was murdered, my health has suffered nor why my sweet mother and precious servants of God that I know fight cancer, and some lose the battle to win the war. I don't understand why children suffer atrocities and things that just don't go as they should… and I am sure that Job wondered too. He said I know you God and I know you know me in my comings and goings so in this I shall trust You too.

Why? That's the question of the meantime, but the answer is here - meanwhile, wait patiently for the Master. Oh, if we could truly grasp this. Be patient in the waiting; with confidence knowing that He is coming and the day is drawing ever closer. Don't complain about others who don't do as they should. Let that be between them and God. Your metal test is the maturity of patiently waiting. I admit that I have a long way to go in this and "meanwhile" is awfully mean to me. The thing we must remember is that God cares down to the very last detail even when we do not think He's there. Let the rain of that storm do its work deep down in you. Be like the seed - quietly storing the storm for the moment God calls you into action and fruitfulness... for He has great plans for you. Don't quit. Find your staying power and dig in because this task before you is enormously worthy. Honor God through it all. It may be days, weeks, months, years or decades that you wait, but store it up. Let that slow, sure work bring patience into your life, and through that patience, work the work of the Master until He comes. Don't waver. He has a plan and He knows the details. It is a good plan to prosper you and bring about good for His purpose. Job waited years and lost much but God blessed him in double portions for his waiting. Let's name those who waited through trials: Abraham and Sarah, Noah, Elijah, Moses, Samuel (Hannah), Esther, Ruth, Joseph, David....Paul, Peter, James, Jesus...wow, easy to see now? In the meanwhile, we learn a lot of who He is and who we are. So cherish that meantime, embrace it for the purpose of storing up His love and depth in you.

Light, space, zest- that's God! So, with Him on my side I'm fearless, afraid of no one and nothing.Listen, God, I'm calling at the top of my lungs: "Be good to me! Answer me!"
When my heart whispered, "Seek God," my whole being replied, "I'm seeking Him!" Stay with God! Take heart. Don't quit. I'll say it again: Stay with God.
Psalms 27:1, 7, 14

Take Heart!

This morning as I laid on the couch on my heat pack, my puppy wanted to be on the couch with me so badly that nothing could detract him. He loves treats, he loves being outside, especially when my husband calls "squirrel"...but today, he has his mind set that I was all he wanted, just to be near me. Wes tried his best to distract him even making him go outside but as he whined louder and louder, I could hear God saying that is how He wants us to desire His presence; realizing that with Him all things are possible and fulfilled. God wants us to desire His presence over all so much that we seek Him with our whole being. God is Light that pierces the darkest of situations and He is space to give us room to breathe in Him and He is zest to give us beauty for ashes and joie de vivre. When your whole body quakes in pain and your heart feels like it cannot take anything else, remember to take Heart and seek Him for He is there. Don't quit. Stay with God!

God is the antithesis to fear so with Him you can be fearless, open, filled with light, space and zest. Scream out to Him. Call out to Him quietly. Either way, He hears you. He's as close as the mention of His name and in His presence all your problems are minuscule.

"You don't have to wait for the End. I am, right now, Resurrection and Life. The one who believes in me, even though he or she dies, will live. And everyone who lives be-lieving in Me does not ultimately die at all. Do you believe this?"
John 11:25-26

The End!

In a story a happy ending suggests a new beginning. This is exactly what Jesus was telling us in John's gospel. The End is the beginning of a new thing. I am one who always wondered what life was like in Happily Ever After...The End. Jesus tells us that He goes to prepare a place for us so that when He returns, He can take us home to this glorious place but He also says we don't have to wait for The End because He is here right now. In this text He was speaking to Martha in regards to her response to His question about resurrection.

Martha had just lost her brother and was a little put out with Jesus because she had called for Him to come before her brother died, but he took too long (in her opinion) and missed the window for the miracle. Oh, how I have often been like Martha – demanding that God do the impossible miracle on my time table so that I would not suffer any consequences; but if only I could grasp that The Resurrection lives in me! The Life, The Word, The Creator of all Mankind dwells in me! Then the suffering and consequences of life are not a mere mortal event, but an awakening permanence in me. Everyone who lives believing in Christ does not die at all, but rather changes residence.

It is so hard to understand this in our mortal scale but if we can but glimpse the moment we are in as a shadow in this world with everlasting consequences for eternity..we would understand that things that seem permanent here are but temporal. Jesus says" I am, right now, Resurrection and Life." There is no need to wait for Him with bated breath as He is here right now. Yes, Heaven is a place of rest and we will be reunited there with those we love who have gone on before but Right Now....the Resurrection is calling you to LIFE! He is calling you to awaken and sing His praises again.

"The accumulated sorrows of your exile will dissipate I, your God, will get rid of them for you. You've carried those burdens long enough. At the same time, I'll get rid of all those who've made your life miserable. I'll heal the maimed; I'll bring home the homeless. In the very countries where they were hated they will be venerated. On Judgment Day I'll bring you back home a great family gathering! You'll be famous and honored all over the world. You'll see it with your own eyes-all those painful partings turned into reunions!" God's Promise. Zephaniah 3:18-20

What a Day!

Reunions and family gatherings have changed a lot since so many have gone on home. I love the words in Zephaniah, for it is simply stated as God's promise. Accumulation of sorrows dissipate like the fog before God's breath. Burdens that weighed us down and people who made us miserable are gotten rid of by Him at the same time. The sick and maimed healed; the homeless brought into an eternal home. In the countries where they are hated, they will be honored. On Judgement Day, it will be a family reunion that surpasses anything we've ever seen because all the painful partings will be reunions with loved ones as we are honored and made famous all over the world.

God's promises! But listen again-He says You've carried those burdens long enough-stop! I, your God, will get rid of those burdens if you give them to me. Rest in Him. Quit trying to carry a load that He is able and willing to bear. We have carried guilt, pain, emotional baggage and situational packages of doubt and fear for so long now that it is affecting our ability to be what he wants for us. He wants freedom for us! He wants lightness and confidence and trust. He wants to carry us! But first we must yield to His desires for us.

If we act like recalcitrant children demanding our own ways, He cannot do for us what He desires. Yield to Him today for He cares for you and desires to carry your load. Sorrows of your separation will dissipate as the morning dew – this is God's promise.

Take good counsel and accept correction- that's the way to live wisely and well. We humans keep brainstorming options and plans, but God's purpose prevails.
Proverbs
19:20-21

Smarty Pants!

In our human nature, we think that we are so smart that sometimes we cause ourselves more problems. I was reading a story about a lady who had called the police to say that she had been shot. She was sitting in her car as the officer walked up and she said that she had been shot in the back of her head, and was holding what she thought was her brains leaking out (Ugh!).

The police officer looked in the car and saw no blood, he asked her to lift her hands and he found a ton of dough on the back of her head from a biscuit can that had exploded in her backseat and struck her. The story shows how we have limited perception of our reality, as we don't always see the truth for what it is. This is why in Proverbs we are advised to take good counsel because we often are short on wisdom.

We keep trying to figure out our own ways because we as humans think we can find ways around the issues that we are constantly conjuring up; but God's plan will prevail – no matter what people put in His way, no matter what politicians say, no matter what the government says. God is superior and only his plan will prevail. So we must rest in that and quit allowing the tos and fros of nature to affect us. Don't let the situations and ups/downs of life to toss us around when we are His children, the sheep of His pasture…His beloved.

There is nothing that He would not do for us and we must have confidence that whatever storm or trial we are going through, He will take care of us.

When I consider Your heavens, the work of Your fingers, The moon and the stars, which You have ordained, What is man that You are mindful of him, And the son of man that You visit him?
Psalms 8:3-4

Consider the Heavens!

Looking around as I was driving, I saw a woman standing on the side of the road holding a "help" sign, indicating she was homeless. God spoke deep into my heart that so many wander this Earth undecided and inconsiderate of their eternal home...they are wandering in wealth and fancy cars, but on their heart is a sign reading "Help! I'm Homeless!"

God sees each and every sparrow and knows each and every need. He doesn't consider one man over another in terms of eternity...He is mindful of all. When is the last time you considered the heavens and the work of God's hands? Just thinking of all that wonder and where we fit into it is mind boggling, but knowing He considers His plans for us intimately should raise us up in understanding His complete love for us. He spoke everything into existence; He made man and breathed His own breath into us!

Why aren't we more mindful of Him? Each morning I get a notice on my phone to breathe deeply and mindfully meditate. Why? Because it is widely known that spending time in the presence of the Almighty brings peace and reduces stress. If God is so mindful of each of us, why are we not more mindful of Him?

Can we honestly count the amount of time spent focused on Him? Are we spending more time worrying and fretting about what us or isn't than we are in worship? What sign are we holding up for others to see - Help! I'm homeless or Hallelujah I'm homeward bound? How can I help you find an eternity with the Savior and precious home in glory? Who are you, or who am I, that a King would bleed and die for us?

Live creatively, friends. If someone falls into sin, forgivingly restore him, saving your critical comments for yourself. You might be needing forgiveness before the day's out. Stoop down and reach out to those who are oppressed. Share their burdens, and so complete Christ's law. If you think you are too good for that, you are badly deceived. Make a careful exploration of who you are and the work you have been given, and then sink yourself into that. Don't be impressed with yourself. Don't compare yourself with others. Each of you must take responsibility for doing the creative best you can with your own life.

Galatians 6:1-5

Creative Life!

Defining creativity is more than looking it up in a dictionary because God's definition is much more robust and not found in Webster's dictionary.

Sometimes I look around and see the creativity of others and I feel a lack in myself; then I hear others say how creative they think I am. The truth is that God defines our creative lives, not us. Creativity isn't defined in a singular way. Each of us has been given creative talents that are unlike any other, but God has defined the creative life He wants us to lead through a few easy approaches to opening our hearts/minds to Him.

Let's explore!

1. Forgivingly restore those who have sinned, saving your critical comments for yourself.

2. Stoop down and reach out to those who are oppressed, share their burdens and fulfill the law of Christ.

3. Make careful exploration of the work/ministry laid before you and of who you are, then sink yourself into that ministry as unto God.

4. Neither be impressed with yourself, nor feel less than, by comparison to others.

5. Take responsibility for doing the creative best you can with your own life.

"I am the Vine, you are the branches. When you're joined with Me and I with you, the relation intimate and organic, the harvest is sure to be abundant. Separated, you can't produce a thing. Anyone who separates from Me is deadwood, gathered up and thrown on the bonfire. But if you make yourselves at home with Me and my words are at home in you, you can be sure that whatever you ask will be listened to and acted upon. This is how My Father shows who He is-when you produce grapes, when you mature as My disciples.
John 15:5-8

Deadwood Floating!

Wes and I love to collect driftwood because we think it is pretty and we put it into our gardens where it can once again connect with life that is teeming in the ground. Floating in the river or ocean current, carried from hither to yon, a branch is drifting towards certain destruction and pointless meandering, pulled along the tide or current with no purpose, soon to be dashed against the rocks and broken. This is how many of us go through life; floating or meandering along, bemoaning our lack of life's fullness, envying others who seem to have it all.

Jesus gave us purpose and placement. He charged us with a supreme duty and responsibility of remaining IN Him intimately and organically. Don't miss this - the abiding in Him is the secret to life. This is what leads to harvest, fruitfulness and most importantly the organic intimacy with Christ. Organic - natural, no falseness, no additives, no fakes, pure, real...this is what being joined with Christ is all about. People can try to fake it, but intimacy is a place of confident authority. A secure place of truth with no doubt. Walking in complete confirmation of who God is despite what the circumstances say. God's words at home in us.

What does that mean? The Word is God. He spoke "Light" and there was light. Being at home in His word means complete confidence that whatever you ask will be listened to and acted upon. I can promise you it doesn't always look like you think it will, but it does happen. So which do you choose to be - deadwood aimed to be burned or beaten/broken by the world, or a fruit producing vine anchored in His love and words, deeply rooted so that no stormy gale tears you away to toss you into the fires? It doesn't mean you won't have troubles.

There are always troubles, but Jesus said "Be of Good Cheer". We can be confident that He has overcome all of them. Isn't it time to take your deadwood - from floating along, tossed in the river of life - and give it purpose again by plugging back into the life-vine?

"Don't look for shortcuts to God. The market is flooded with surefire, easygoing formulas for a successful life that can be practiced in your spare time. Don't fall for that stuff, even though crowds of people do. The way to life--to God! is vigorous and requires total attention.
Matthew 7:13-14

Shortcuts!

The washing machine, the dishwasher and the microwave are but a few of the amazing technologies we have that help us shortcut the chores in our life. The technological advances to make our lives easier and more seamless have abounded in the last few decades . Sometimes we think there is a shortcut to everything from health to weight loss to our relationship with God, but this isn't the truth. I was hurting last night...I was really hurting last night. I hardly slept, until early this morning.

The reason is because I was not feeling well, but also because I was in an intensive spiritual battle. By nature, I'm a lover not a fighter. I love to embrace people with the love of Christ and show them His amazing and wondrous works but the truth is that Jesus could have taken a shortcut and He didn't. Jesus could have called the angels down and never suffered the shame, indignity and pain of the worst possible death a man has ever known, but He chose to drink the cup of iniquity for us and lay down His life for our sins. What greater love? His path to the cross wasn't a lackadaisical journey, but rather one filled with wondrous purpose - from the manger to the Heavens. He didn't stay in a grave; He arose victorious. I think of His battle in the Garden of Gethsemane where He asked His close companions to have His back and battle with Him, but night overtook them and they fell asleep.

There are loads of self-help books out there on every topic under the sun - from how to find natural plants for meds to how to make yourself a millionaire - but yet, the only book that carries the story of His extreme love and sacrifice is falling by the wayside. We have gotten so far from His word that we only digest a morsel or two when a Bible app pops up on our phone. How can we expect to survive a battle on a crumb of food that has fallen rather than eating at The King's table of His choicest and finest that He gives us? A battle is not something you can ignore. It may have weapons that are not of man's making, although some men have made vicious biological weapons. This battle, like the Battle of Gethsemane, is not for the faint of heart, nor for the one who only wants a snack to fuel him. This battle belongs to God and He is calling our warriors who desire life to its fullest. He's calling us to complete and vigorous attention. The weapons are not man-made, but spiritual. The battle lines are drawn.

Satan has declared war on the Saints of God and is attacking on every front. Will you engage? Will you begin to spend time, attention and your vigor on the things of God so that you are prepared to wage battle or will you simply sit on the sidelines with popcorn hoping to join the winning team, throwing out suggestions and advice from the latest book or podcast? It is time to gear up and wage spiritual battle on our knees, walking our floors, claiming our victories, because we already know Who has won the war - but there are no shortcuts!

Don't love the world's ways. Don't love the world's goods. Love of the world squeezes out love for the Father. Practically everything that goes on in the world-- wanting your own way, wanting everything for yourself, wanting to appear important-has nothing to do with the Father.
It just isolates you from Him.
The world and all its wanting, wanting, wanting is on the way out-but whoever does what God wants is set for eternity.
1 John 2:15-17

The Wants!

My, we are a greedy people! The King of all Creation gave His only Son for us; Jesus gave His life for us and all we can think about is what we want – from the next meal, to healings, to deliverance, to movement in our everyday life. Yes, I have been walking floors in prayer and dwelling with God until He spoke this simple question: Daughter, why do you love me?

Of course, I am like Peter and all the other disciples, responding that I love you because you are God and you are so good to me. Jesus didn't ask them Why, but rather Do you love me? Me, he asked why. The tender answer was a barb and a truth. As I answer...I love you and I want more of you Lord, He spoke – always filled with the wants. Then I was directed to read this scripture. Oh how ashamed I am for always going into prayer with wants. How can one know they are loved for who they are if all you ever do is ask them to do something for you?

The truth is that we are a spoiled people wanting God for His works and magnificent ways rather than just because of who He is. He wants the intimacy of a deep love, a true love. He knows us and loves us as we are but oh the depths of that love when we love Him just for who He is and not because of what He does.

Don't love the world's ways (the have-it-your-way psychology), but rather learn to live as His. Learn to love and walk in love because of who He is not because of what He does. Love of things in this world squeezes out the love of the Father. Love of things, money, wealth, fame, popularity, success...love of self-always filled with wants, always looking at what others have and you don't, etc....all this wanting...this is not of God. God loved. Period. He loved. He didn't send His son to be sacrificed for your sins because He wanted to provide you a genie in a bottle. He sent His son because He loved you and wanted to bridge the great divide that became a gulf because of the I wants. Lucifer was cast from Heaven because of the I wants. Eve was tricked into eating the forbidden fruit because she was selfish and pursued the I wants. Adam ate after her because of his I wants...and continuing throughout scripture, the I wants of worldly selfishness lead to a path of destruction.

The yielding Is when the yoke Is broken, salvation comes and deliverance Is met. Esau wanted and lost his birthright. David wanted and murdered a man for it ending in great grief; but God's forgiveness and His willingness to sacrifice for us all was clearly seen in the Garden of Gethsemane where the battle was won in prayer...when Jesus yielded His flesh through the sweating of drops of blood as He said, "not my will but thine be done." This...this is the laying down of the I wants. Today I challenge you to pursue God passionately despite your pain, your desires, your wants. Put them aside and pursue Him simply because of who He is, not because of what He does.

They said, "If you will be a servant to this people, be considerate of their needs and respond with compassion, work things out with them, they'll end up doing anything for you." But he rejected the counsel of the elders and asked the young men he'd grown up with who were now currying his favor, "What do you think?"
2 Chronicles 10:7-9

Rejecting Counsel!

Hearing the voice of God amidst the clamorous noise of life is challenging because it requires that you shut out all and go before Him in stillness. God's voice is a voice of wisdom and comes through His word, but it is also spoken through those of the ages who have lived and steeped in Him over the years. Oh the folly of Rehoboam - who was given a massive kingdom - raised in opulence and wisdom, but failed to recognize God's voice and lost it all. He failed to see the counsel of the Godly saint as the voice of God. The people were frustrated but came to the king in recognition of his father's authority and wisdom that had reigned under the hand of anointing of God. In his youth and folly, he disdained the counsel of the aged in favor of the counsel of the untried and his kingdom was lost. This is the bride of Christ now.

The bride is preparing for the coming of her bridegroom, and yet hearing many voices around her. The untried voices of youth clamor for the latest and greatest in the sanctuary of the Almighty while the counsel of the aged and tried saint is spurned. God directs His anointing through many - both young and old - but He will not tolerate His voice being silenced in the church. The new untried voice is not that of God but rather an insidious poison hiding as a wolf in sheep's clothing. Rejecting the counsel of the aged and steeped in Godly wisdom is folly for they know His voice and can recognize it. I have always listened for God's voice through others for He shares His wisdom this way but it is also important to recognize those who know Him intimately and those who do not. Scripture tells us that we are known by our fruits. If we demonstrate the fruits of the Spirit in our lives throughout our trials, this is how we are known.

Wise counsel doesn't usually tickle your ears but rather is a firm confirmation of, or an indictment against, that which you lean upon. Wise counsel is not given to curry favor but rather to confirm the direction of God or to redirect you to a certain path or purpose. Rehoboam was sadly misdirected because he failed to regard wise counsel and instead followed those who favored him. Be warned that those who fawn over you are not your true counselors.

A true counselor offers to pray for you and will offer sage advice when God directs, but they will not play into your self-esteem as this is not God's way. In these last days many - even the very elect - will be deceived by those who fawn and praise them and hug their necks while stabbing them in the back. Turn away from those who praise and worship you to those who praise and worship the one true God, for it is these wise souls who keep the wicks trimmed and the oil of God flowing. True counsel comes from those who wait upon the Lord to renew their strength. These are they who will rise up on wings as eagles and run without weariness in the path God sets before them. Hear the voice of God. Seek His counsel among those who are fruit-filled.

So, what do you think? With God on our side like this, how can we lose? If God didn't hesitate to put everything on the line for us, embracing our condition and exposing Himself to the worst by sending His own Son, is there anything else He wouldn't gladly and freely do for us? And who would dare tangle with God by messing with one of God's chosen?

Who would dare even to point a finger? The One who died for us-who was raised to life for us! is in the presence of God at this very moment sticking up for us. Do you think anyone is going to be able to drive a wedge between us and Christ's love for us? There is no way! Not trouble, not hard times, not hatred, not hunger not homelessness, not bullying threats, not backstabbing, not even the worst sins listed in Scripture: They kill us in cold blood because they hate You.

We're sitting ducks; they pick us off one by one. None of this fazes us because Jesus loves us. I'm absolutely convinced that nothing - nothing living or dead, angelic or demonic, today or tomorrow, high or low, thinkable or unthinkable absolutely nothing can get between us and God's love because of the way that Jesus our Master has embraced us.

Romans 8:31-39

Our side!

Red rover, red rover, let Jesus come over!

Just thinking about how often we play this game in our heads and hearts instead of realizing that God never left our side. He put everything on the line for us including His own Son, knowing our condition. He exposed Himself to sin, willingly taking it on via the cross for our salvation. He was the bridge across the divide that we created. We forget that He is our champion. In the times of old, He was known by His works as they were broadcasted about and people knew to be wary of crossing the people of God because it would invoke His wrath but now we don't trust Him and we do not expound upon His goodness, faithfulness and protection; so those who walk in evil have no fear of God. If we truly had the conviction of Paul as he wrote this epistle – that absolutely nothing keeps us from God's love – we would approach our living differently.

Instead, we fear for this mortal body. We place more value on our flesh than our soul. I can almost pity Satan for he has set up himself a most powerful enemy when he touches one of God's people. Think…he couldn't touch Job until God allowed it. Why did God allow it? For His purpose and His glory, all things are done. Christ loved us so much that He willingly died for us, so why do we question His authority? God himself fights for us so why do we worry so? Because we are not convinced. We doubt, fear and worry because we see God as we see ourselves-limited, unreliable, wishy washy…susceptible to man's desires and follies. But God isn't man. If we can only grasp who He truly is then our doubt and fear would fade.

Once we truly begin to understand who He is, we can become thankful for the storms of life because it is only through the storms that we understand the value of the Peace speaker. It is only when we walk through tough times that we draw close enough to Him to understand who He is. It is only through trials that we begin to see the victory. If we never want, never struggle, never need, then we never realize who He truly is. The Garden is proof of this-in perfection, we wanted more. The Israelites are the proof of this – in Canaan they wanted a king. We are proof of this for when things are going well, we forget who He is. Red rover, red rover – time for you to turn it all over to Him and let Him be who He is.

I saw the Lord sitting on a throne-high, exalted! and the train of his robes filled the Temple. Angel-seraphs hovered above Him, each with six wings. With two wings they covered their faces, with two their feet, and with two they flew. And they called back and forth one to the other, Holy, Holy, Holy is God-of-the-Angel. Armies. His bright glory fills the whole earth.

The foundations trembled at the sound of the angel voices, and then the whole house filled with smoke. I said, "Doom! It's Doomsday! I'm as good as dead! Every word I've ever spoken is tainted- blasphemous even! And the people I live with talk the same way, using words that corrupt and desecrate. And here I've looked God in the face! The King! God-of-the-Angel-Armies!"

Then one of the angel-seraphs flew to me. He held a live coal that he had taken with tongs from the altar. He touched my mouth with the coal and said, "Look. This coal has touched your lips. Gone your guilt, your sins wiped out."

And then I heard the voice of the Master: "Whom shall I send? Who will go for us?" spoke up, Send me!"

Isaiah
6:1-8

I saw...

There is an ever-present attack upon the ministers of the gospel as never before because they are willing to see God for who He truly is and stand boldly declaring His truths. People are back-talking, lying, slandering and invoking evil wrath upon the men of God because of their own guilt. Isaiah saw the Lord in a vision and every word he had spoken felt blasphemous in his mouth until the Angel of the Lord sanctified his lips with a live coal from the altar of God (the anointing), and then when God called for one who would go, he went forth. The foundations of the Earth tremble today in anticipation of His soon return.

His very elect are preparing for His return, as they are the Bride. The level of intensity of attack upon ministry, both lay persons and preachers, will intensify as never before. A great outpouring of the last days of miracles and signs/wonders will begin soon because we are in the last stages of the pregnancy of time. I can hear the movement of the angels wings as they prepare for the midnight cry – the rapture of the Church – Jesus is coming soon. The urgency of people as they prepare for an incoming storm, such as a hurricane, is palatable. All of nature is preparing, for we are all aware of His imminent arrival. But where are the workers? Where is the church? Are we sleeping or preparing? Are we so weary with the fighting so that we have no energy left to watch? Are we battle weary or battle ready?

Gone is your guilt. Your sins are wiped away when you allow the cleansing of your lips from the impure thoughts, words and deeds. Today I hear a voice from Heaven warning those who would attack the men and women of God's holiness. Beware those who sit behind a keyboard filling their tongues with tainted language and the hearts and minds with a lying spirit. Beware, for you will not be forgiven an assault upon God's beloved after you have been offered the coal of cleansing fire. While you may think you are righteous in your ways, there is none righteous, no not one, save he/she be blood-bought and their lips cleansed with the anointed coal from God's altar. Do not touch God's beloved in word or deed, lest you reap coals upon your head. False prophets say God is a God of love and would not send His anger towards someone but that is not who God is. God is the same yesterday as He is today, as He will be tomorrow. He is unfathomable, untainted and cannot be changed. He is the I Am. He will not be shaken.

"I'm telling you these things while I'm still living with you.
The Friend, the Holy Spirit whom the Father will send at my request, will make everything plain to you. He will remind you of all the things I have told you. I'm leaving you well and whole. That's my parting gift to you. Peace. I don't leave you the way you're used to being left-feeling abandoned, bereft. So don't be upset. Don't be distraught.
John 14:25-27

Well and Whole!

As I sit here trying to recover from sickness, my heart's desire is to be well and whole. This is the longing of every heart-to be at peace, to feel whole and complete and to be well. A well is a hole made in the ground to access a source of water, usually from a natural spring. I venture to say that digging a well deep within us to the core of who we are and allowing the Spring of Living Water to dwell there gives the sense of completeness like no other.

The completeness of Jesus In our lives Is the peace He speaks of In John's gospel. The Holy Spirit keeps us in perfect peace as our mind stays on Him. It's a quiet conviction, a knowing that no matter what, He is in control. There is no feeling of being left alone because you are not alone. There is no feeling of being abandoned because you are not without. Are there disappointments and trials? Absolutely. This world is not our forever home and these bodies are not made for eternity but we are.

We are eternal souls resting for a time in Earthly portals until Jesus comes to take us home again. The moth in this picture is a thing of rare beauty but the moth was first a caterpillar then cocooned in the knowledge that he was being changed. He knew who he was as a caterpillar on the ground eating leaves and he knows who he is as a moth lighting on leaves/flowers. His outer looks have changed but he is the same. A moth only lives a few days to a few months. His purpose is clear and he knows what he is to do.

They flutter about achieving their tasks and bringing beauty and life in the doing because they know their purpose and go after it with all that is in them; this is direction. Jesus said that he was saying these things so that we would be well and whole. He left us with purpose. A job to do, a high calling to tell others about His peace and this was His gift to us. While our bodies may suffer from infections and viruses, our spirits have been given peace and life through Christ Jesus.

Here's how you test for the genuine Spirit of God. Everyone who confesses openly his faith in Jesus Christ -the Son of God, who came as an actual flesh-and-blood person- comes from God and belongs to God. And everyone who refuses to confess faith in Jesus has nothing in common with God. This is the spirit of antichrist that you heard was coming. Well, here it is, sooner than we thought! My dear children, you come from God and belong to God. You have already won a big victory over those false teachers, for the Spirit in you is far stronger than anything in the world. These people belong to the Christ-denying world.

They talk the world's language and the world eats it up. But we come from God and belong to God. Anyone who knows God understands us and listens. The person who has nothing to do with God will, of course, not listen to us. This is another test for telling the Spirit of Truth from the spirit of deception.
1 John 4:2-6

Spirit Test!

It's that time of year where pep rallies and cheering for your team is a demonstration of your school spirit. People run out to buy the latest in school promotional wear and get excited to be attending games of sports involving their teams. From crazy socks to backwards clothes, students and teachers as well as parents and community show their support by wearing certain items and showing up to support their teams. Genuine spirit involves support, but there are many who could care less who will participate to fit in.

The same thing can be the case in "the church" as far as the spirit so in John we are instructed on how to recognize the genuine from the false. The spirit of the antichrist talks a good game, even spouts religious philosophy and professes to be of God but they will not acknowledge openly that Jesus Christ is the only way – that He came as God in the flesh. He was God, is God, and always will be...God. Scripture says that in Him dwells the fullness of the Godhead bodily. If they refuse to confess that Jesus is the only way, truth & life then they are not of God. The Christ denying world accepts multiple gods/religious authorities and the false teachers teach that God loves all but won't judge all, even those who openly live in sin. This is a false religion with its roots anchored in hell itself. You cannot serve two masters. The way to discern the spirit of deceit from the Spirit of Truth is by telling The Truth-scripture untwisted and untarnished.

Those who are of God will listen and learn. Those who have a false spirit will turn away, argue or attack you as being fake or judgmental. The Spirit of Truth in you will acknowledge the truth and affirm it in your hearts and minds. Anyone who knows God will understand and listen to His words. This is a spiritual battleground but you have already won a big victory because the Spirit that raised Christ from the dead lives in you. Fear is not of God. Faith is of God. The Spirit who lives in us is stronger than anything in this world!

I'm glad in God, far happier than you would ever guess-happy that you're again showing such strong concern for me. Not that you ever quit praying and thinking about me. You just had no chance to show it. Actually, I don't have a sense of needing anything personally. I've learned by now to be quite content whatever my circumstances. I'm just as happy with little as with much, with much as with little. I've found the recipe for being happy whether full or hungry, hands full or hands empty. Whatever I have, wherever I am, I can make it through anything in the One who makes me who I am. I don't mean that your help didn't mean a lot to me-it did. It was a beautiful thing that you came alongside me in my troubles.

Philippians 4:10-14

Quiet & Content!

"Whatever I have, wherever I am, I can make it through anything in the One who makes me who I am." What a statement! Paul made this statement to the Philippians. He didn't say that God gave him this ability. He said he learned it. He said I have learned by now to be quite content whatever my circumstances-happy with little as with much. This place of quiet in the spirit is a learned skill from walking through circumstances of life and seeing God's Providence. A place of being glad in God – far happier than people would guess – is a choice, despite the circumstances; not because of them. A quiet spirit is a confident spirit. It isn't inactivity but rather stillness. I think of a duck sitting quietly on the water and yet underneath the surface his little feet are paddling. He projects a feeling of quiet stillness and yet he is actively moving. This should be us in the Living. We should be confident as Paul states and yet actively seeking the lost-Knowing that all our labor is for His purpose. Learning to rest in quiet confidence while being about His business means that we are walking in Him.

Happiness is the golden ticket that everyone seeks. Thousands of dollars are spent by advertisements promising happiness with their product. Millions of hours are spent seeking what is readily available for the learning. It isn't an instant gratification but rather a steady walk that gets you to the place of contentment. The difference in contention and contentment is vast and learned.

"These words I speak to you are not incidental additions to your life, homeowner improvements to your standard of living. They are foundational words, words to build a life on. If you work these words into your life, you are like a smart carpenter who built his house on solid rock. Rain poured down, the river flooded, a tornado hit - but nothing moved that house.
It was fixed to the rock.
Matthew 7:24-25

Set in stone!

As I was cleaning my ring, I noticed that the setting was still just as strong as the day it was made. This is because the foundation is solid all the way around. I remember when the jeweler was making the ring and he said the light couldn't get to the diamond with the framework I had designed.

I told him that the security of the diamond was more important to me than it sparkling everywhere. Foundational truths are things to build upon so when times are shaky and uncertain, one can remain calm and in control. With recent storms and high winds, it is easy to understand that if you fix your house to a strong foundation then it can withstand the stormy gales. God's words are set in stone. They are a strong anchor, a place that will not be moved. His words form a foundation to the world as His words spoke the worlds into existence and by His words all can cease to exist. There is none like Him.

He Is a rare jewel, a masterpiece that Is unwavering In its certainty. As I see strong storms that come and move homes from their foundations, I think of Him and how nothing can move us from the palm of His hand. We are His. Nothing will be shaken in us that we anchor to Him.

Nothing and no one is holy like God, no rock mountain like our God. Don't dare talk pretentiously- not a word of boasting, ever! For God knows what's going on. He takes the measure of everything that happens. The weapons of the strong are smashed to pieces, while the weak are infused with fresh strength. The well-fed are out begging in the streets for crusts, while the hungry are getting second helpings. The barren woman has a houseful of children, while the mother of many is bereft.
1 Samuel 2:2-5

Infused!

Each time I have gotten sick or had surgery, I look forward to getting a vitamin infusion to restore my blood levels. I have a friend who owns an infusion company and it is beneficial to get this dose of vitamins and minerals, as your body has been depleted. It gives you an immune boost and makes you stronger. My mother gets them weekly after chemo to restore her cells. Food/nutrition is what reading the Word is for our spiritual health and going to church is like getting an immune boost. It strengthens you for the battle ahead. Each day our physical bodies battle invisible, ever-present bacteria and viruses on the surfaces of things we touch and our spiritual bodies battle the same way-invisible forces of evil that crowd our world/hearts/minds.

We wrestle not against flesh and blood but against principalities of evil in high places. Never has this been more evident than in these end times. We are confident that the battle is won and Jesus is victorious but we must continue to fight. Our physical bodies are strong, but they weaken when too many things assail it at once...sometimes we have to get antibiotics. These recognized enemies of our body strengthen our immune system by telling it to produce more warrior cells and fight harder-like a battle cry. God allows adversity to come at us to strengthen our battle readiness and make us stand a little stronger, produce more fruit, strengthen our boundaries and cry out to Him for reinforcement. Our God isn't like any other. He knows the exact measure of everything that happens and He allows the weapons of the strong to be smashed so the weak can be infused with His strength. He allows the well-fed to go without so the hungry can get nourished. He allows the barren to have children as the mother of many sees her children grown and gone. Why does God allow these things? Cancer & sickness, pain & disease? Because they are all tools to get us to call for reinforcements and to pull us into the spiritual battlefield. Too long we fight, we get tired in the waiting, but God says we will rise up with wings like eagles.

They that wait on the Lord...will renew their strength...they will be infused with new power to rise up to battle. Come to His word for an infusion of rich vitamins and minerals. Taste of His living water. View the battlefield you are facing as an opportunity to stoke the fires hotter, fan the flames to burnish those weapons, and let the antibodies build you back up. Let the attacks against the body of Christ be as antibiotics calling out the warriors of the immune system to recognize the enemy for what it is and fight harder; call upon the name of Jesus and fight, for the gates of hell cannot prevail against those who stand arm in arm with the God of all! Don't boast or talk pretentiously! Speak God's power and authority! Nothing and no one can outsmart our God! There is nothing or no one as strong and mighty as our God... call to battle!

In prayer there is a connection between what God does and what you do. You can't get forgiveness from God, for instance, without also forgiving others. If you refuse to do your part, you cut yourself off from God's part. "When you practice some appetite-denying discipline to better concentrate on God, don't make a production out of it. It might turn you into a small-time celebrity but it won't make you a saint. If you 'go into training' inwardly, act normal outwardly. Shampoo and comb your hair, brush your teeth, wash your face. God doesn't require attention-getting devices. He won't overlook what you are doing; He'll reward you well.
Matthew 6:14-18

Training Rules!

When people decide it is time to get their life on track, whether physically, mentally and/or spiritually, there is often a demarcation point upon which the change in them is remarkable. From weight loss/fitness to mental health/ brain training to spiritual fruits, change is evident when a person puts forth effort to make a difference. Jesus is saying here that there is a definite connection between what God does and the effort we put forth. You cannot ask for & expect forgiveness if you are unwilling to forgive. If you refuse to do the necessary work to make change, then change cannot happen. The mental/physical/spiritual are all tied up together. But when you begin to try to discipline your inner self to gain hold and concentrate more on God, it is important that the focus doesn't shift to you and your sacrifice or your method/means when the purpose is all about getting to know God more intimately.

The purpose Isn't to draw attention to yourself but rather to focus on Him and allow Him to do the work in you while you also discipline yourself through the fasting experience. Fasting has turned into a fad or stage of physical discipline instead of being the spiritual discipline that God called for it to me. There are mega fad diets and physicians who have caught the wave of the benefits of fasting to the physical body and partner it with mediation instead of prayer. Yes, there are benefits to fasting and meditation (which is really another way to say prayer and be politically correct), but if your mind isn't centered on God and it is centered on you then you miss the best purpose of all which is to discipline yourself into a place of supplication and hearing God's voice. It's not a show or a fad, but rather a way to tune your station to the one that you should be hearing. It's not about the music, the weight loss, the healthy feeling nor even about the sacrifice of time…it's about finding the wavelength of God's anointing and resting in it with complete abandon. Find your time with God. Your "appetite-denying" discipline may not be food. It may be Facebook or other media, video games or TV, or books or any number of things. The point is to identify what appetizer is stealing your attention away from the main course of God's instructions. What is filling your belly so much that you don't have time for the main course? I love a good appetizer, especially those chips/salsa but I am always full when the main course arrives because I always enjoy the chips/salsa too much. Then the meat dish arrives but I have no appetite to enjoy it. This is what God is saying in these scriptures. Discipline yourself to pay attention to Him and to prepare for His divination to you of the things He has for you to learn. Discipline yourself to be at church. Discipline yourself to be in prayer. Discipline yourself to get in His word and swim in it deeply, not just a shallow scripture or two. Get dressed and be about God's business in everything you do. Go about your normal day and your normal tasks while learning to meditate on Him. Find that time with Him can be intimately yours and then allow the Sprit to draw you closer to Him.

Where is the god who can compare with you - wiping the slate clean of guilt, Turning a blind eye, a deaf ear, to the past sins of your purged and precious people? You don't nurse your anger and don't stay angry long, for mercy is your specialty. That's what you love most. And compassion is on its way to us. You'll stamp out our wrongdoing. You'll sink our sins to the bottom of the ocean. You'll stay true to your word to Father Jacob and continue the compassion you showed Grandfather Abraham - Everything you promised our ancestors from a long time ago.
Micah 7:18-20

Awesome God!

Yom Kippur is a Jewish Day of Atonement. It is the day to reach out to any person whom you may have wronged and clear the air, ask for forgiveness and make things right. We should do this every day. God doesn't reserve one day a year to clear our slates and wipe away our sin with a tidal wave of His love. He puts the sins forever away and they are not acknowledged any more. His mercy and compassion are fresh and anew constantly for us. True, He doesn't tolerate wrongdoing, and sin is an abomination to Him, but He is true to what He promised to His people and to those who came after...His compassion will not fade.

In Colorado Springs, there is a beautiful area of rocks called The Garden of the Gods; but it should be called The Garden of God, for it is a place of beautiful, majestic stones that are awe-inspiring. People come from all over to see these rocks...rocks that cannot cry out or do anything but stand there. They are worth seeing, but each time I see these, or The Grand Canyon, or many other wonders around the world – wonderful works of God - I cannot help but think of His statement that if we will not praise Him, the rocks will cry out. I think of the times in the Bible where a donkey spoke or another inanimate object was given voice or life simply by His whisper. How magnificent is our God that He allows us compassion and mercy. He allows us forgiveness and praise. He allows us what belongs to Him. He is so willing to forgive and reach out to us...what are we doing with His gift? Are we allowing the rocks to shudder and moan around us readying themselves to give voice of praise to the Almighty because we are too busy praising other people and things that are undeserving of our praise? How we spend celebrating others when He deserves our praise!

"Trivialize even the smallest item in God's Law and you will only have trivialized yourself.
But take it seriously, show the way for others, and you will find honor in the kingdom. Unless you do far better than the Pharisees in the matters of right living, you won't know the first thing about entering the kingdom.
Matthew
5:19-20

Famous!

Each year as we got ready for field-day trips, we had T-shirts printed identifying which students belonged to which teacher's group. When I got my group assigned, I would tell them to remember who they represented and to conduct themselves as my representative. By then they knew me - both tolerations and expectations. The same can be said now of my employees who represent my business, which reflects who I am. I took my husband's name when we married and as such am a representative of our family, just as our children are as they have been taught.

We as Christians take on the name of Christ. The word Christian means Christ-like. In His name we have all the authority that He established through His death and resurrection. Authority to speak to mountains to move out of the way, devils to flee, illness to go, storms to cease and the power to invoke change in lives by leading others to Him; these are all ours through His name! Those are the amazing privileges that come with His name.

With great privilege, comes great responsibility also. We represent the King of Glory. There are protocols to royal behavior. I admit I am a little bit of a royal watcher mainly because of the pomp and circumstance. There are certain things that can and cannot be done when you represent the kingdom. These rules or commandments are written and strictly followed. Those in line for the throne, as well as those surrounding them, must agree to these protocols in order to be allowed to represent the royal court, even if they were born into the privilege, but especially if they married into it. The honor they receive is given because they represent something much bigger than themselves. If they trivialize one small detail, it could affect the decorum and upset the monarchy resulting in sanctions or loss of privilege/status/authority as we have seen in recent times. The commandment is "Do not take the Lord's name in vain." In vain means for vanity or lightly or without purpose or intent. Often this command has been taken as one just should not curse or use God's name in slang (that too!). My brother shared an insight - if you take the name of Jesus Christ by calling yourself a Christian, you are His representative and all that you do is in His authority and gracious permission of representation.

This means that by claiming to be a Christian you are claiming to belong to Him-taking His name. If you fail to represent Him in word, deed or action and instead represent yourself purposefully doing things not in line with who He is, then you took His name in vain. Wait...what? That's correct. You take His name in vain when you comport yourself outside His nature, laws, expectations, because you represent Him If you call yourself a Christian. Weigh that - we have His authority which carries this responsibility.

There are a lot of smooth-talking con artists loose in the world who refuse to believe that Jesus Christ was truly human, a flesh-and-blood human being. Give them their true title: Deceiver! Antichrist! And be very careful around them so you don't lose out on what we've worked so diligently in together; I want you to get every reward you have coming to you. Anyone who gets so progressive in his thinking that he walks out on the teaching of Christ, walks out on God. But whoever stays with the teaching, stays faithful to both the Father and the Son. If anyone shows up who doesn't hold to this teaching, don't invite him in and give him the run of the place. That would just give him a platform to perpetuate his evil ways, making you his partner.

2 John 1:7-11

54

Invited In!

Who and what are you inviting into your life? John wrote to the church about those voices set up to deceive and ruin lives. He wrote for us to beware of the spirits of deceitfulness and the antichrist. False doctrine can often be misconstrued as progressivism. Thoughts like "We need to reject certain aspects of scripture to be progressive" are lies from Satan. Accepting that which is false and that which is against God's word does not make you progressive, but rather full of deceit. I am astounded by how many insidious technologies are now aimed at mind-washing our children and young adults into the lies of Satan and the antichrist in the guise of progressive thought. Demonic witchcraft in cartoons and then people arguing that the cartoon is aimed at young adults doesn't make it okay. The rapid acceptance of that which is satanic and demonic in our culture as main stream from homeschooling groups that train kids to be witches to commonplace occurrences of homosexuality in every single show on TV. Pedophiles now openly talk about their mental disorder and sin as if it is acceptable on talk shows and sitcoms.

Our culture has sacrificed the innocence of the unborn on the altar of convenience and the minds of our children in the worship of technology. I was surprised to see a recent study that said children believe social media and YouTube 40% more than they trust their parents. This means that our youth and our future has now been given over to a deceiving liberal media who has fed our children lies about everything, but we spend more time on the ball fields than we do in the house of God – our children see where our priorities are. They see what we say with our lives. They see what we say by where we put our time, money and effort. They see that the dollar is more important than God in our culture and our lives. They see how much time we spend in the Word of God and prayer. They see when we are sick that we first rush to doctors/science instead of The Great Physician. Understand I am not against social media, convenient things nor doctors. I use all of these but the Where and the Who and the What we prioritize matters! What spirit are you inviting into your home with what you watch and read and play? Who are you giving place to in your life through where you place your mind and thoughts? Are you focusing on God and His promises or allowing doubt, fear, frustration, anger, bitterness, etc. to ruin your marriage and family? Where are you spending your time and money; the house of God, or entertainment?

Do your kids know what is a priority to you? Ask them. They will tell you the truth. Rev Don Brankel used to say if you want to know where your priorities are, look at your checkbook. So, look at where you are spending your time and money; for that's who, or what, you've invited into your life. Who's partner are you? Are you partnering with evil ways instead of your spouse? Spending more time on the iPhone or the TV than with the one you say you love? Are you praying, or complaining? Are you watching the signs of the times with prayer and supplication or are you to busy whining about what you don't have, while you covet what others have? Are you letting oppressive spirits of depression get inside your head with negative thoughts and insidious evil or are you capturing those thoughts and surrounding yourself in God's word?

I look around the floors and see dirt has gotten tracked in so I pick up the vacuum and begin to remove it. This is the same thing you must do when dirty words/thoughts/deeds get tracked into your mind by other things passing by you. Don't entertain them and make mud pies with that dirt. Suck it out and then empty the container in the garbage. Wash those nasty clothes that stink with the sweat of the day and wash your mind with the blood of Jesus. You are not immune to the dirt, muck, and germs of society but you do get to choose what you do with it. Boost that immune system with the Word and pray. Strengthen the fighting power of your mind by mediation on what is good, what is lovely, and what is of good report. Do not entertain the stinking thinking! Wash that grey right out of your hair and that muck right out of your thoughts! Now go clean your spirit house, for today God would like to dine with you!

Make this your common practice: Confess your sins to each other and pray for each other so that you can live together whole and healed. The prayer of a person living right with God is something powerful to be reckoned with. Elijah, for instance, human just like us, prayed hard that it wouldn't rain, and it didn't - not a drop for three and a half years. Then he prayed that it would rain, and it did. The showers came and everything started growing again.
James 5:16-18

Powerful Prayer!

The key to powerful prayer is clearly laid out in this passage. First, we must make it a common practice, which means to do it so regularly that it has become a habit. Secondly, we must confess our sins to one another and pray for each other so that living together whole and healed is possible. Third, live right with God. If we do the first one then the second and third are easy because they come with the practice.

If you practice praying and believing, then the living clean and praying for others is natural, which is then followed by living right before God. Elijah made a habit of prayer and knew his prayer availed much, so when his helper told him there was a cloud the size of a man's hand, he told him to run because rain was on the way. Whether the powerful rain came from the little cloud or if that cloud ballooned into many clouds matters not to me. What matters is that Elijah kept praying and believing until he saw the evidence of the cloud then he knew the result was on its way. This is the same helper that God removed the scales from his eyes so he could see God's army. The fact is that seeing is believing in our world, but sometimes we allow the scales of the world to hide God's truth from us and only by prayer can we get a clear vision.

The other day my husband got a splinter in his eye and although it was tiny, it blocked his vision. I worked hard getting that splinter out of his eye, washing and washing it and using what things I had on hand. His eye is still irritated some from that experience. When we fail to protect our worldview from the doubt/fear that influences the world around us, we become sighted to the splinter and our vision is affected. We must remove the splinter of doubt and fear through intense constant prayer so that we can see the common practice of living water flowing over our vision, washing us so we can see!

"You're blessed when you get your inside world - your mind and heart - put right. Then you can see God in the outside world.
Matthew 5:8

Input-Output!

"Input-output, what goes in must come out! Input-output that is what it's all about! Input-output, your mind is a computer whose input-output data you must choose!"

This is a fun song that I teach my students for realizing that negativity can affect your outlook on life. In Matthew, Jesus says the blessing of getting your mind/heart aligned with God is that then you can see Him around you in your everyday world. It's truly all about choice.

When we choose to put God first, He aligns everything in Him. It's the measure, the standard, the goal to which you align that keeps your focus where it needs to be – the priority of your mind and heart. If your priorities in your mind and heart are right with God, then your outside, everyday world will align with Him. When you get twisted up in other things, then your priorities get misaligned and you get all tangled up. We are infinite beings fixed into a finite body and when our minds align with this body instead of God's purpose and eternity, we start focusing on keeping this body happy in the present instead of aligning with our eternal purpose, allowing the God of eternity to manage the finiteness of our mortality.

Our God of wonder sees far beyond our galaxy when our minds can barely grasp the moon and stars. When you survey all the beauty that surrounds you in nature, it is much easier to begin to understand the infinity of God; but when you focus on the immediate, it's like focusing on the leaves falling to the ground. You get stuck in a mindset of time passing and what you are missing or lacking. Take a moment, shift your focus, see His infinite mercy and grace. Look beyond your circumstances to where He is. Count your blessings and His favor. When you get your input right, your output will be much better for everyone around you.

Everything was created through Him; nothing not one thing! _ came into being without Him. What came into existence was Life, and the Life was Light to live by. The Life-Light blazed out of the darkness; the darkness couldn't put it out.
John 1:3-5

Life-Light!

At the birth of a child, it is like a light flipping on, into incredible brightness! When I look at the two wonderful young men whom I birthed, I am amazed that God chose me to be the vessel to bring them to His world. All of nature is amazing in its creation, but none is as fascinating to me as the wonder of a child. Jesus is the Life-Light that blazed out of the darkness and could not be put out and each child born is a life-light.

This is why the evil darkness works so hard to quench life in the womb, because evil knows this. Each time a child is born, a piece of Heaven is placed on Earth. Our supreme purpose is to worship our Creator, which draws more Life-Light into our world. This photo of Niagara Falls is one place I have always wanted to see but have not as of yet. It is a place of seemingly infinite and incredible wonder and power. It intrigues the mind with the vastness and reach, but it is only one small wonder of nature, even with its vastness. God establishes each life-light with purpose to bring light into the surroundings of that life.

That is the purpose of each of us. We are to bring light to those around us. I am thankful today for my life-light, my spouse's life-light and for the two life-lights we were blessed to raise. God is so good as He allows the life-lights to expand. Now both my boys have met and embraced the beautiful women who will continue the life-light.

Remember: A stingy planter gets a stingy crop; a lavish planter gets a lavish crop: I want each of you to take plenty of time to think it over, and make up your own mind what you will give that will protect you against sob stories and arm-twisting. God loves it when the giver delights in the giving. God can pour on the blessings in astonishing ways so that you're ready for anything and everything more than just ready to do what needs to be done. As one psalmist puts it, He throws caution to the winds, giving to the needy in reckless abandon.

His right-living, right-giving ways never run out, never wear out. This most generous God who gives seed to the farmer that becomes bread for your meals is more than extravagant with you. He gives you something you can then give away, which grows into full-formed lives, robust in God, wealthy in every way, so that you can be generous in every way, producing with us great praise to God.
2 Corinthians 9:6-11

Lavish Crop!

When grass or a crop grows, it has no boundaries except those that are put on it by others. If you plant only a little, barely investing of yourself, then you'll reap only a little. Better to be wise and invest prolifically in the things of eternity with certain return than to foolishly throw time and money away in the wishes, ifs and should-haves. Your willingness to invest of yourself into the Kingdom of God is tied to the return you reap. If you invest with a grudging heart, then you'll reap grudgingly... with little joy. If you invest with cheer and thanksgiving, then your return is bountiful and brings happiness. If God is to throw caution to the wind, giving to you in reckless abandon so that you are ready for anything and everything, then you first must demonstrate that you are ready for that type of giving by being an open vessel.

His provision to you is directly related to the flow. If He has given you a place of service, even if it seems menial, unimportant, or unnoteworthy (mowing yards, scrubbing toilets, nursery duty), then do that thing with joy and excitement; for that us your place of calling, your investment into eternity, and your opportunity to be His hands. A river doesn't start as a river. It starts with a single drop. A mud-hole can become a living stream teaming with life through God's blessings of living waters if that mudhole is willing to be more than what it is. It requires investors. It requires willingness. It requires consistency because sometimes digging the path is a muddy and unappreciated job. Maybe you feel like you are in the sewer and everything you do is stinky and mucky. Remember that God has purpose for that place. Dig it out. Allow that nastiness to become washed in His glory and become fertilizer rather than just waste. It's your choice: wallow in the muck or begin to use it for His glory.

Are you a river or a mudhole? Have you become a like beaver that works to stop the flow, so consumed with yourself and your wants that you are shutting off the blessings in your life and those around you by your actions, words, deeds? Are you damming up every gift God gives or are you generous and sacrificial? Are you giving with abandon and cheer or are you a grudging, griping mess? God loves a cheerful giver, not a whining petulant brat who gives only because it is expected. He wants to bless you lavishly with rivers of living water, but if you are so focused on yourself that you dam up every opportunity with a bad attitude, angry actions and selfish mindset, then He will not bless you, nor will He continue to tolerate it. The storehouse is full. He wants you to be blessed. Open your heart to others. Give lavishly of yourself and of your means so that God can flow through you to others!

Start with God - the first step in learning is bowing down to God; only fools thumb their noses at such wisdom and learning.
Proverbs 1:7

The First Step!

Solomon is historically known as the wisest king to rule in ancient times. His wisdom was widely known because his wisdom was God given. When God favored him by asking him the one thing He could give him above all else, anything he desired, Solomon asked for wisdom. This touched God's heart. This young man who could ask for ANYTHING, asked after God's heart. God gave him his desire and everything else too-wealth, health, etc., because he had asked for what God desired in him. You see, Solomon recognized and then put in writing for us; the key to all our heart's desires – start with God. I've watched so many people kick and scream and beat at closed doors when all along they had the key in their hand, but they are too foolish to use it.

The other day, I got out of my car, put my key ring on my hand and loaded my arms down (doesn't take much these days as I cannot carry much due to my back), then tried to open the door, only to realize it was locked. So, I started kicking the door, banging it with my head and elbow, trying to get someone's attention to come open it, when all along I had the keys in my hand! All I had to do was put the other things down and use the key instead of becoming frustrated that no one was opening the door for me. This is a picture of us using our worldly ways and means to approach the throne of God with our needs. We have our hands so full of wants, desires and selfish needs that we kick and scream at the door of wisdom to allow us access while all the time holding the keys in our hand. We must be willing to lay it all down for His sake, for His glory. This is the first step. Lay it all down/bow down to His will in your life and quit kicking at the door. It will only open when you are willing to start with Him. We live in a world of fools who try their best to ascertain who God is in order to be a god through wealth and riches, to demand their own way in a world created by God himself. They thumb their noses at the simplistic viewpoint of using the key to unlock the door as they stand banging, screaming, kicking and demanding access to something they will never know because they refuse to lay down their idols and their own flesh in submission to their Creator.

Every knee will bow and every tongue will confess but it is too late once He closes the door. Access is then denied. Picture this! Jesus is standing right by you at the door saying I have given you the ability to walk through, given you the key to unlock the door, just lay down those selfish ambitions and unlock the door as I stand right here at the door willing to carry those burdens for you and give you all the desires of your heart – all you gotta do is give them to Me. My husband walked around the garage door and saw me with my hands full. He chastised me for taking on too much, then he willing took the load for me so I could unlock the door. He had been out working as he heard me losing my every-loving cool, so he left his work to come rescue me. This is the picture of Jesus. Unburdened, I was able to use the key. My husband couldn't do it for me. The key was on my arm under all the packages. I had to give them to him to access the key to unlock the door. As I finally opened the door, I turned back around to get the packages insisting that he give them to me as he asked why. Why would I want to carry those burdens again when he had them? He was more than capable and had already walked through the door with me carrying them.

I hope you are catching this; let Jesus satisfy your soul. Give Him those burdens so you can give access to the rest He has promised you. Allow Him to be your strength. He's enough. You don't have to do it on your own. Start with God!

"It's urgent that you listen carefully to this: Anyone here who believes what I am saying right now and aligns himself with the Father, who has in fact put me in charge, has at this very moment the real, lasting life and is no longer condemned to be an outsider. This person has taken a giant step from the world of the dead to the world of the living.
John 5:24

Alignment!

My steering was a wobbly mess as I tried to drive. The gauges said things were ok and when I looked at my tires, they appeared ok – inflated, with plenty of tread. Honestly, I was stumped. Things didn't feel right, but everything looked ok.
So I asked my husband to look and drive my vehicle. He knew instantly what the problem was – misalignment. I took the vehicle in and got an alignment with new tires because the front-end caused wear on the inside of the tires which made them dangerous to drive on, potentially a blow-out scenario.

It's urgent that we listen carefully to what God is saying and align ourselves with the Father through the measure of Christ Jesus. The difference in walking through life feeling off and out of step, to complete confidence and knowing, is alignment with Him. I'm not a mechanic and know nothing about tires, but I knew something was wrong when I was driving because it felt off. There is an internal feeling we get when things are not in alignment with Him. It's like walking with a limp or having a cut that prevents you from functioning fully...it's a sense of feeling off.

When I cut papers at the office, I use a guide that aligns the paper so I can cut it quickly and accurately. If the pages are not aligned correctly, they end up asymmetrical. Jesus is our guide to full alignment with the Father. It is through Him that we can find directions to our lives and the how in our functioning.

In this all-out match against sin, others have suffered far worse than you, to say nothing of what Jesus went through all that bloodshed! So don't feel sorry for yourselves. Or have you forgotten how good parents treat children, and that God regards you as his children? My dear child, don't shrug off God's discipline, but don't be crushed by it either. It's the child He loves that He disciplines; the child He embraces, He also corrects. God is educating you; that's why you must never drop out. He's treating you as dear children. This trouble you're in isn't punishment; it's training, the normal experience of children. Only irresponsible parents leave children to fend for themselves. Would you prefer an irresponsible God? We respect our own parents for training and not spoiling us, so why not embrace God's training so we can truly live? While we were children, our parents did what seemed best to them. But God is doing what is best for us, training us to live God's holy best. At the time, discipline isn't much fun. It always feels like it's going against the grain. Later, of course, it pays off big-time, for it's the well-trained who find themselves mature in their relationship with God.

Hebrews 12:4-11

God's Training!

Have you ever expected one thing and gotten another, which disappointed you? I reason that we all have at some point. The likelihood of this happening is high, because we set our expectations on our beliefs or desires, which don't always transfer to the way others do things. At my office we use personal brain trainers because we want people to be pushed to their very best level of training – it is unmatched by any other type of training. In life, we are in an all-out match against sin and we need the best training to prepare us to stand against the forces of evil and to not give in.

The trials you are in and the disappointments you experience may seem as if God has let you down or given up on you, but I ask you to reconsider them through a new perspective – the lenses of training. A parent who has never changed a dirty baby diaper is a hilarious thing to watch. I'll never forget watching my husband change our eldest son's first diaper as I tried my best to instruct him from the hospital bed. I laughed so hard my sides hurt. He used an entire container of baby wipes on one diaper change. That was the beginning of his training. He was shoved right into the experience and had to learn through the dirtiness. Sometimes life is like that. God sends or allows things to come our way that we feel is like tar stuck on our foot. We cannot seem to get away from that thorn, but God is instructing us from the sidelines through His word – if we take the time to listen or read the instructions. I am fascinated by the General Sherman tree in this picture. It has stood for eons of time, slowly growing into the giant it is today. It has watched seasons changed and storms come and go, like many of our church elders who have learned through life's training ground.

Both this tree and our elders have learned that time with God changes all things and that seasons of life change. The training ground is forever. We are always learning and growing; as long as we are willing to engage. When we decide to sit on the sidelines, we still get the trials and the tests based on our previous training. If you feel like you are stuck in a rut, quit just spinning your wheels. Spend some time with God and allow Him to instruct you on getting out of those ruts – this is the training ground through defined intimacy and authority in Him. Allow Him to train you to become the warrior that He desires you to be, so that you can be a quick learner; remember, everything has a season.

Your time of winning and resting comes too. Breathe, and trust God! Discipline isn't fun, but it makes for great training. No discipline equals lots of tests which you fail and struggle with – learning the hard way. Decide to take the time for learning through Him and applying the principles so that the training ground leads to quick learning in that season. A seasoned warrior is the kind who has learned that everything has a time and this too shall pass, as he/she battles through it in Faith through Christ Jesus. Give it all and don't give up! He truly has purpose through it.

One final word of counsel, friends. Keep a sharp eye out for those who take bits and pieces of the teaching that you learned and then use them to make trouble. Give these people a wide berth. They have no intention of living for our Master Christ. They're only in this for what they can get out of it, and aren't above using pious sweet talk to dupe unsuspecting innocents.
Romans 16:17-18

Sharp Eyes!

Words of counsel or wisdom come from those who have experienced it and learned. In Romans 16, Paul is concluding his letter and thanking those who have been there for him, but also those whom he persecuted in the previous life as they stood strong in their faith. His wisdom is this: keep a sharp eye out for people who use bits and pieces of scripture to prop up their beliefs/ teachings, as they are only trying to stir trouble and not truly aiming for the mark of the high calling. They use the words, but have no intentions of really following through. I see this all the time in the business world where people use the language, but have no depth or follow- through.

They pray in a pious manner, saying the words you want to hear, but then they have no truth when their actions follow through. The life of a believer speaks volumes above the words; believer who is wise knows that there are many who use the "lingo" to capture those who are unsuspecting or new to the calling. It is our job to nurture baby Christians and support them. It is terribly hard to live a fruitful life without others around you to pollinate and support you with the love and admonition of the Lord. Notice I said admonition because most of us like the love, but the constructive criticism is hard to bear.

This beautiful picture is a reflection in the water of homes in the glory of fall, shown here in the trees. It is beautiful and it reflects the true picture, which is even more beautiful. The point is that beauty and love reflect in our lives when we walk in the true nature of who Jesus is. Jesus said, "come unto Me all who are weary and I will give you rest." Are you being a reflection of who Christ is in your life? Are you keeping sharp eyes out for those set to deceive and mentoring those who are in need?? Are you giving wide berth to those who use Christ as a soapbox that they never open to wash themselves?

Are you listening in love, advising in God's word and walking in His counsel (reading the word) daily? These are checkpoints, not criticisms. These are goalposts to help you keep a sharp eye on the path ahead of you.

Every God-born person conquers the world's ways. The conquering power that brings the world to its knees is our faith. The person who wins out over the world's ways is simply the one who believes Jesus is the Son of God.
1 John 5:4-5

Conquering Power!

I have several friends who hike or climb mountains as a workout or a relief, and others friends who conquer life's mountains through the same means. What's the difference? One is just a path through which we exercise our bodies, while the other is a test we overcome by pushing past our own preconceived limitations. God proclaimed that through faith we have the power to conquer the world and bring it to its knees, and that faith is within us, but most of us only exercise that faith through minor exertions of our faith. Those who walk through the trials that are deep and arduous are those who conquer the mountains of the world's ways and begin to walk in big faith. Walking big and conquering doesn't always look like we think it will. Sometimes that conquering power is the winning out over death, hell and the grave through the conquering faith of transition from this life into the next. That faith is the ultimate faith of the believers. It is the eternal Blessed Hope that Christ has promised. Conquering the world's ways and bringing the world to its knees is through simple faith, and it is done in prayer and praise. The way of the world is a way of plodding and hopelessness, except in the powers that be who have money, wealth and fame.

The way of faith is a simple confidence that He has it all under control no matter your circumstances, through any and all storms. Conquering a mountain means pressing past the limitations you have set on yourself and your abilities; it is very exhilarating, but conquering the mountain through faith requires you pushing past the limitations you have set on God and begin to believe that He can do more than you ask or think. Our finite minds limit our own abilities and ever more limit what we believe God can do. What if? What if you allowed Faith to bring you to the place of unlimited power and unlimited release of your troubles to God? What if you truly leaned in and allowed Him to be God fully and completely in your life? What power could be had in allowing Him to be who He said He is! What confidence! What joy! What completeness!

But…God is who He says He is, whether you choose to believe it or not. The difference is in hiking or conquering. Are you just hiking the mountains of life and exercising little faith or are you conquering those mountains by pushing past the limitations of who you believe God is into the impossible?

God, my shepherd! I don't need a thing. You have bedded me down in lush meadows, you find me quiet pools to drink from. True to your word, you let me catch my breath and send me in the right direction.

Even when the way goes through Death Valley, I'm not afraid when you walk at my side. Your trusty shepherd's crook makes me feel secure. You serve me a six-course dinner right in front of my enemies.

You revive my drooping head; my cup brims with blessing. Your beauty and love chase after me every day of my life. I'm back home in the house of God for the rest of my life.

Psalms 23:1-6

Reviver!

Are you in the place of contention, or in the place of contentment?
Traveling across this country, there is plenty of beauty to be seen; I can understand how the psalmist said beauty and love chase after us, because God's beautiful love is etched into the skies morning and night, no matter where you live. What David discovered in his pursuit/career of being a shepherd was that God has an eye ahead and knows where we are headed, even when we don't. He takes us through places of trial and growth, darkness and death. He leads us through rough patches and away from what looks like the best of things because He is taking us through to a better place…a place of complete rest, joy, and contentment.

What He desires from us is the simple trust of the sheep for the shepherd. The sheep only see what's in front of them; the shepherd directs or leads them. As long as their eyes are to the ground looking at what's immediately there, they may get disgusted or disappointed because it's not lush, green grass at the time. The world is filled with dead emptiness, where the locusts have destroyed the crops and fields, but The Good Shepherd wants us to lift our heads from the place of contention and grief to see the place ahead…a place of rest and reviving. He is the lifter of our heads who sees beyond what we see and knows what is ahead. He prepares us for the beauty and for the hard times if we will lean in to Him.

He sets a full course meal Of His word in front of us daily; that is enough to sustain us through the lean times… if we will grasp His infinite provisions. The cup He pours for us is not skimpy or "iffy", it is filled to the brim with His blessings; but as long as our eyes are looking down at the ground we are standing on, we cannot see His blessings and provisions. We wander off in our own path; counting our sorrows and regrets, rather than our blessings and our salvation. How do you know when God is truly your shepherd? When you have allowed Him to be fully yours, you can say…. I don't need a thing!

God, I am content in the place I am, though I may have walked through death's valley and lost the loved one who once walked with me. I am content because I trust that I can see Your provisions around me, despite the path I am standing in now. I know I can trust Your rod and staff - your shepherd's crook - to redirect me to Your path, from which I have wandered away. I know I am home in the house of God for life, no matter what the circumstances say. God, you are my Shepherd and I will not fear that which is before me because I know You have prepared my path. God, I don't need a thing because You are my provider!

On the final and climactic day of the Feast, Jesus took his stand. He cried out, "If anyone thirsts, let him come to Me and drink. Rivers of living water will brim and spill out of the depths of anyone who believes in me this way, just as the Scripture says." (He said this in regard to the Spirit, whom those who believed in Him were about to receive. The Spirit had not yet been given because Jesus had not yet been glorified.)
John 7:37-39

The Final Climax!

When you are reading. Every book has a turning point; a juncture that changes the story forever – that point in the story is called a climax. Jesus lived out His life on Earth and there was a final climax…His death. That was the end of the story according to man, but it was truly a turning point for the believers. On that final day, when Jesus spoke, He gave us instructions that direct us every single day of our lives as we live in Him. Those instructions tell us that if anyone thirsts, let him come to Jesus and drink. The promise is real! Once you have taken a drink of the living water you will begin to fill up on life and flow with living water - into the lives of others. That is the climax of all climaxes! Once you reach that turning point in your life, surrendering your life fully to Christ, the Holy Spirit comes and takes up residence. You will have a hunger and thirst for more of God, and more of God, and more of God… until you immerse yourself in the rivers of God. Once you are immersed, those rivers begin to flow in you, through you, to you and for you; those rivers of life and living water become rivers of power and might, directed by faith into the lives of others, changing the direction and the course of everything you do. You see, a river that takes on extra water from its tributaries begins to change the course of the land around it.

The power of water is one of the strongest forces on earth. Hurricanes form over water and reform landscapes by their might. I understand the power of a mighty river, but the power of living water flowing through you can change the landscape of your life forever if you will allow it to fully flow and quit damming it up it in your life by lack of belief.

Lord, I believe all things are possible! All things! Not some things, all things!

"This exile is just like the days of Noah for me: I promised then that the waters of Noah would never again flood the earth.
I'm promising now no more anger, no more dressing you down. For even if the mountains walk away and the hills fall to pieces, My love won't walk away from you, My covenant commitment of peace won't fall apart." The God who has compassion on you says so.
Isaiah 54:9-10

God says so!

The carbon monoxide detector went off in the middle of the night, sparking flames of irritation that come from being startled awake. It wasn't that dangerous gas levels were detected, but rather a weak battery was found to be the issue. And, it didn't matter that the batteries were replaced, it still kept beeping because it needed to be reset. The incessant action of this inanimate object caused tempers to flare further until the device was removed. In this verse of scripture, God is speaking to the Israelites about their incessant sin and the exile He had allowed because of their constant willfulness. Then He issues a promise of no more exiles, just like the promise of no more flooding. Most importantly, He promises no more anger, no more dressing them down. He promises an everlasting love and a covenant – a commitment of peace. Oh, that promises of no more anger and frustration flareups were possible in our lives!

The God of compassion knows our hurt and frustration because the Israelites had continually sinned against Him, as we have; He is awoken to our constant, incessant beeping in our prayers of need for relief-protection-provision. How frustrating must it be to be constantly in demand to meet the needs of others and yet those same people rarely take the time to meet your needs. What a patient God that He hears us and responds to our incessant demands when we fail to acknowledge His ways or His goodness as we should. What a magnificent God who always rises on our behalf, never becoming angry at us, nor striking out at us, when we rarely acknowledge His goodness, provision and authority. What an amazing God who lights the sky by day and night providing for us in ways we cannot fathom before we even think to ask, and yet we are not even mindful of what He is doing, nor doing as He asks us to do. When is the last time we truly got before God in thanksgiving and praise without a single request for our own needs, wants or desires? When is the last time we sacrificed our time, money, desires for Him without a thought towards a return investment from Him? He is jealous of us. He desires our worship, our praise, and our commitment. He desires that we be as constant to Him as He is to us.

God's anger will be kindled again in judgement for a broken covenant of peace made by other nations against Israel. God has promised peace to Israel and the incessant pull against His promise by other nations is wearing His patience thin. His wrath is on slow burn against the nations who continue to thwart His will despite His constant redirecting, but this is not a message of doom...it is a message of hope. God says so! The God, who has compassion on us, says so! What a powerful statement! He says even if the mountains crumble away into the sea, His love is there. He has committed to peace and constancy in love to us for eternity. I love a rainbow because it reflects God's promises.

God's promises are real, true, fixed – on Him and in Him. I have had plenty of times that a promise or a person's word to me has been broken. I have lots of hurt and disappointments, but I can truthfully say that God has never failed to be there for me nor has His loving peace ever failed to wrap around me when I was in need. Even to the end of times, His love and peace will continually dwell with us even we fail Him. How do we know this? The God who has compassion on us says so!

Blessed be God- - He heard me praying. He proved He's on my side; I've thrown my lot in with Him. Now I'm jumping for joy, and shouting and singing my thanks to Him.
Psalms 28:6-7

Thrown In with God!

Things don't always go the way we want them to go! Life is never just, but God is. Life is never fair, but God is. He's continually proven that He is on my side, despite my circumstances or my concerns. He's proven himself true over and over, even when I doubted Him or failed Him. Throwing a lot in means jumping in with all that you are; abandoning your own wants, needs and desires for His, knowing that He has you… no matter what. The jumping for joy, shouting and singing of thanks doesn't come because life is perfect, but because He is faithful and just in our circumstances no matter what the reports of others say! Doctors, lawyers, politicians, and economists may say things look bleak, but I know that greater is He who is in me that all of these in the world. I don't put my trust in what stands before me, but rather in the Creator of the universe. I will not allow myself to become beat down, nor destroyed by circumstances, because He is greater than my biggest need! He sees the big and the small. He knows me better than I know myself. I haven't seen everything, done everything, known everything, nor experienced everything, but I know a God who has seen and still sees it all, has known and still knows it all and has felt and still feels it all.

He has never failed me, even if things didn't go the way I thought they would, or should. If life seems unfair and everything or everyone seems to be letting you down, I'd like to introduce you to this friend of mine – I give you Jesus. Jesus… the Peace that passes all understanding, the perfect Love that casts out all fear, the Water that you'll drink and never thirst again, The Counselor, The Mighty God, The Prince of Peace, The Mighty Fortress, The Deliverer, The Lion of Judah… moreover, His name is LIFE! If you feel lost in the shuffle, needing some answers, feeling regret, measuring your letdowns, come meet this friend.

God met me more than halfway, He freed me from my anxious fears. Look at Him; give Him your warmest smile. Never hide your feelings from Him.
When I was desperate, I called out, and God got me out of a tight spot. Is anyone crying for help? God is listening, ready to rescue you. If your heart is broken, you'll find God right there; it you're kicked in the gut, He'll help you catch your breath, Disciples so often get into trouble; still,
God is there every time
Psalms 34:4-6. 17-19

Shades of God!

As I stepped out into the breaking dawn, I looked over and saw the color shades of fall everywhere, as well as the shades of drought. It can be hard to discern the autumn colors unless you are very observant, or are married to an outdoors guy! The fact is that we all have seasons in our lives, and in those seasons of drought and loss, struggles and losing, we still have the same opportunity to look like shades of gold to others. The turning of the leaves is a sign of not enough sun and sometimes not enough water, but it is a thing of beauty. Trees that are not evergreens must shed their leaves in order to store and preserve the tree in winter. They grow deeper in drought rather than taller and wider. They have less to give to outer branches, so the leaves fall to the ground and become fertilizer for the undergrowth and food for the tree itself as they break down into compost. God is listening. He hears you in every season of your life. Sometimes those seasons look bleak and you just cannot understand the why. But, if you look to Him and give Him your anxious fears, He will hear you and free you from them. He will make your season a golden season of beauty and help you catch your breath. We often get into trouble - often of our own doing - but as His disciples, He is still there for us every time. Never hide your feelings from Him. He's ready to help and wants to be your provider and source. He is God! He is your Father!

Raise a Hallelujah!

Heaven is described to us as having streets of gold. This picture also has a street of gold. This road is covered in golden leaves - fallen from aspen trees. The sun still peeks through the trees and illuminates the leaves, a sparkling road that reminds me that seasons of life change; we change with them, but change can be beautiful, even in pain. Things may look rough, but look up to Him; give Him your anxious fears and allow Him to turn your sorrows into joy and your failures and griefs into streets of gold for those around you to be led to Him. What if today we choose to be shades of God's glory, forming streets of gold through our struggles so others may come to know Him and, in return, we experience growth and goodness in the depths of His Sonshine? Shades of God surround us in all the seasons of our lives; we just need to look up!

If I give everything I own to the poor and even go to the stake to be burned as a martyr, but I don't love, I've gotten nowhere. So, no matter what I say, what I believe, and what I do, I'm bankrupt without love. Love never gives up. Love cares more for others than for self. Love doesn't want what it doesn't have. Love doesn't strut, Doesn't have a swelled head, Doesn't force itself on others, Isn't always "me first," Doesn't fly off the handle, Doesn't keep score of the sins of others, Doesn't revel when others grovel, Takes pleasure in the flowering of truth, Puts up with anything, Trusts God always, Always looks for the best, Never looks back,
But keeps going to the end.
1 Corinthians 13:3-7

Truth Flowers!

Roses have always been a sign of love or care; whether given as the bouquet of a first love on Valentine's Day or as an arrangement for a loved one's final resting place...but love doesn't fade like the roses, do nor does it lose its fragrance, shed its bloom, or cast off its petals. Love is constant through the frustration and anger, through the grief and despair, through trials and temptations, through joy and sorrow... through all...love is constant. It doesn't ever give up, get stuck on itself, think it is better than another. Love isn't forced, but natural. Love doesn't remember failures and keep score of downfalls.

Love isn't I-told-you-so or reveling in others' losses. Love is pure wealth. It is the only commodity that cannot be bought nor traded. You cannot make a flower bloom and you cannot make love happen. Love is a flowering truth that bursts from the fertile ground of sacrifice. You must till the soil, plant the seed, constantly water it, and tend it. You must pull the weeds that would steal sunlight, water, and nutrients; you must prune back that which is not fruitful. Love, as a flowering truth, only comes through constancy. It cannot be forced, faked, or duplicated. Love is real, has depth and lasts forever. Marriages fail and people fail. Sin happens and hurt happens.

Love never fails. Love never hurts. Love is timeless and unswerving. Love never gives up. Love cares more for others than self and therefore isn't consumed with self. Take time to read 1 Corinthians 13, the love chapter. Love is the ultimate goal, both the beginning and end... because God is Love. If anger arises, love cannot exist there. Anger is a weed that chokes love. Tend your garden. Nurture your love roses. Make sure that as seasons come and go, you are putting in the effort required to keep your love healthy.

πίστις

For I am not ashamed of the gospel of Christ, for it is the power of God for salvation to everyone who believes, for the Jew first and also for the Greek. For in it the righteousness of God is revealed from faith to faith; as it is written, "The just shall live by faith."
Romans 1:16-17

Still the Same!

When reading the nuggets of God's Word, especially His promises, I like to read them in multiple versions of Bible translations, as well as the original Greek and Hebrew so that I can get a full view and perspective of the Word. These two frames are pictures of the same rainbow, just like the scriptures are different translations of the same text. The Greek word for Faith is pistis. Each time it is used, it has an asterik by it because the word has so many meanings open to interpretation. As I studied this morning, I thought of all the different views of one rainbow and how your perspective of that one thing is different for each person who sees it by location.

A pilot might be flying through that rainbow, seeing it a glorious sense, while some see it in the storm and others before or after the storm. The thing is that God is the same as we live faith to faith. God doesn't change. Our perspectives might. Our version of events or interpretations might change – we view things differently as we age – but God doesn't change! How should we live in these turbulent times? Faith to Faith. This is God's powerful plan to rescue all who believe on Him. The way to right standing before God is in God through Faith. Faith isn't faith until it's all you have. The depth of trust a child has for the parent who responds to every cry is faith. The depth of TRUST we have in Our God who responds to our every need is Faith!

As Paul writes to the Roman church, he realizes they are being persecuted and looked down upon for following a "Hebrew" religion with "Greek" texts and writings, both of which were not respected in that Roman world. Today, walking by Faith, believing that God will isn't a popular opinion, and is scoffed. Some believe He can, but chooses not to, and few believe He WILL – that is where the power that raised Christ from the dead rests. The power of Christ Jesus is in our Faith that we are justified. It isn't of our own making. We spend more time trying to figure out who God is (and will He or won't He?) than we do in prayer! As a boss, I never question whether what I say to do will be done because I know my people and I know they will do exactly as I ask within their own abilities. When I say to do something, I know it will be done, confidently.

When I ask my family to do something, I am confident they will try to do it in their way and time, according to their abilities and willingness. So why do I doubt God? Because I place the same foibles on Him that I do my human counterparts. I wrap Him in my human failures rather than in His character. Get this please – it will change your life. God is God, not human! He came as flesh and dwelt among us so He could show us the pathway of Faith and the power of the anointing. He came as flesh to demonstrate to us that He is beyond the humanity. He is God! You are His! If we only begin to walk in it fully, what miracles will be wrought in our world! The same God that raised Jesus from the grave lives in us! It is time for the bride of Christ to begin to walk in the authority of Jesus Christ who conquered all the world had to offer including fear, death, hell, the grave...He conquered it by walking faith to faith, healing blinded eyes, raising the dead, restoring withered limbs, healing lepers, calming storms and casting out devils. He conquered it all faith to faith through the power of the Word. Walk faith to faith as believers, confident not only that He can, but that He WILL!

So if you're serious about living this new resurrection life with Christ, act like it.
Pursue the things over which Christ presides. Don't shuffle along, eyes to the ground, absorbed with the things right in front of you. Look up, and be alert to what is going on around Christ-that's where the action is. See things from His perspective.
Colossians 3:1-2

Look Up!

I watched a movie not too long ago called "Look Up!". The premise of the show was that an asteroid was hurtling towards the earth, expected to wipe everyone out. The news media and the politicians were telling people that it wasn't going to happen, but if people looked up they could see it coming in the sky. So, the people who knew it was coming went around telling everybody to look up and holding posters that said look up; yet people were so busy with their lives and listening to others that they believed the falseness. I couldn't help but see the paradigm of truth from scripture.

The Earth is not ours to save, but those around us are. The power to change one mind/heart is by pointing them to Christ, telling them to get their eyes off their current circumstances and LOOK UP! Yesterday, as I stood in the mist and the light began to break through, I began to diligently look for the rainbow, as I know the principles of water/light refraction that cause the rainbow spectrum, but I failed to recognize that I was looking beyond the science. Looking up isn't just literal here in this verse, but figuratively also. We must get serious about pursuing the life WITH Christ and run hard after the gifts/purposes/fruit/goals He presides over rather than staying focused on the things of the here and now. It is time for us to begin to be alert to the changes going on around Christ - that's where the action is; start seeing things from His perspective as to what matters. He is not contented with you shuffling along in misery with a what-will-be-will-be attitude! That is not Faith.

He's not content with you drifting and floating along in the Living Water soaking yourself as if you are bathing and relaxing in Him. Yes, there is a time for that-a season. But this oh-well-God's-gonna-do-what He's-gonna-do attitude is not what He has called you to do! So I'm screaming, LOOK ⮝ UP! Both to you and to me. If you want to see God move, then start moving in Him. If you want to see miracles, then start praying and walking in them! If you want to see dry bones come to life in God, then get your arthritic-self up off the couch and get to the house of God. Things are being shaken and stirred. The closer you are to the eye of the hurricane, the more power you experience around you, while being in the midst of peace. The Eye of God is stirring. Get in with Him-See through His view. Allow the power of the Almighty to stir and shake. Everything will be shaken and stirred; are you going to be thrown about off your ways in the midst of the storms or are you stepping into the eye of the storm and experiencing His power/authentic authority around you, through you as you anchor in His perspective?

The fundamental fact of existence is that this trust in God, this faith, is the firm foundation under everything that makes life worth living. It's our handle on what we can't see. The act of faith is what distinguished our ancestors, set them above the crowd. By faith, we see the world called into existence by God's word, what we see created by what we don't see.

Each one of these people of faith died not yet having in hand what was promised, but still believing. How did they do it? They saw it way off in the distance, waved their greeting, and accepted the fact that they were transients in this world. People who live this way make it plain that they are looking for their true home. If they were homesick for the old country, they could have gone back anytime they wanted. But they were after a far better country than that heaven country. You can see why God is so proud of them, and has a City waiting for them.

Not one of these people, even though their lives of faith were exemplary, got their hands on what was promised. God had a better plan for us: that their faith and our faith would come together to make one completed whole, their lives of faith not complete apart from ours.
Hebrews 11:1-3, 13-16, 39-40

Distinguished!

"Fame! I'm going to live forever!
I'm gonna learn how to fly high
I feel it coming together
People will see me and cry
I'm gonna make it to heaven
Light up the sky like a flame
Fame-I'm gonna live forever"

The composer of this song longed for that which was fleeting. His name is not known by most. He had a moment of fame and his life faded. Cancer killed his transient life and fame killed his spiritual life, for he let the desires of the moments here take his eternity. The foundation of faith is the difference that makes life worth living. If one lives only for the here and now, it is fleeting and disappointing. Life is full of ups and downs, but if your foundation is solid, the redecorating, or remaking, is just a process. As a young lady, I just knew I would become a doctor until life happened and those plans changed through a horrible life experience of loss. Then as a teacher/principal/reading specialist, I felt I had achieved a goal, but was still waiting on the rest of my life to unfold. Marriage, children, and many other things have met some of my goals, aspirations and dreams, but they too have come along with life's disappointments. I've had health issues and other ups/downs. Through calling and ministry, I opened a business and have seen huge success, amazing results, and life changes for people, but also discouraging times. Through it all, I've learned that my foundation, through faith, is in God.

God is there through it all, whether I am up or down. Whether I'm flying or crashing, He keeps me. Emotions roll-er-coast, people change, plans fail, things come and go, but life continues. If a person looks only to the immediate of life, it is exhausting. Only in the long look to the eternal-the faith walk – can one truly see what will be. Hebrews 11 is considered the Faith chapter because it recounts the people of Faith who still have Fame, though that was not their goal. What distinguishes a person of God is their Faith-walk. By Faith, Peter stepped out of that boat to walk on the water, but he looked at the waves and allowed fear to steal his victory. He isn't remembered as the one who walked on water, but rather the one who sank because he doubted. This is us. We are people of fear, doubt-filled with anxiety and discouraged by little things; but if we would only keep our eyes on the prize of the higher calling rather than whether our dreams are timely or not, then we would see the world differently as those of Faith did. The world we see everyday was called into existence by a single word. God said Light and there was light. Each of the people of Faith mentioned saw ups/downs, but none of them saw their Faith promise fulfilled. They saw it in the distance through immortal vision-eternity sight: the Faith vision. I watch people who are fascinated with the 3D and 4D goggles that give them a false sense of reality. They put you into a world that seems real through the senses and interactions that feel real via vision, but is false. That's where we are now. The faith of these examples should be our faith, even in the doubt. When Thomas doubted, Jesus allowed him to touch his scars and blessed those who believed but hadn't seen. Though Sarah laughed at the promise of God, it still happened.

As Joseph sat in prison wondering where God was, he refined his faith because he got his eyes off his immediate cir-cumstances and saw the promise afar off. He was raised up into authority and dominion but when he died, he asked for his body to be carried into the promise land because he saw with latter vision. Faith vision doesn't mean that nothing good happens here in life. On the contrary, faith vision opens doors to the impossible. By faith, though some doubted, many things were achieved that others thought impossible: Walls fell, dead were raised, lions tamed and prisons opened. We serve the God of the impos-sible who by a single word sets things in motion, creates life, allows death with eternity awaiting and grants beauty out of ashes. He calms storms, opens blind eyes, heals the lame and turns water into wine just by will. He gave us these same powers and opportunities if we will walk in the Faith He gave us. It's your choice to be extinguished or distinguished. Faith is the difference.

That's why I don't think there's any comparison between the present hard times and the coming good times. The created world itself can hardly wait for what's coming next. Everything in creation is being more or less held back. God reins it in until both creation and all the creatures are ready and can be released at the same moment into the glorious times ahead. Meanwhile, the joyful anticipation deepens.

Romans 8:18-21

Deepening Anticipation!

It's the season of baby showers and birth announcements everywhere. Gender reveals and online announcements of pending birth are daily on the feed and yet these are no comparison to the actual day of the birth. This is why scripture compares this time to the pregnancy of a woman as Earth in travail...breathlessly awaiting. All of nature is in anticipation, but not of the birth of the Messiah, for He has already come and lived among us. The anticipation now is for His arrival as King to catch His bride away. I remember all the preparation and anticipation of the wedding...the dress, the photos, the ring, the special moments...all leading up to the celebration of the union. As dawn begins to break, the birds begin to chirp, announcing the news of the new day. The breathless anticipation and excitement they have is felt in that first chirp that immediately is followed by a chorus. The sky is still dark, but that first glimpse of a ray of light brings that hope.

In these verses, Paul is writing about our unbelievable inheritance and the opportunity of reigning with Jesus. He knows the hard times and has experienced them, but he sees that first crack of dawn and has begun to notify others that Christ's promises are true and real and present and on their way. It feels like forever as I sit watching that first hint of light harkened by that chirp... it feels like forever until the dawn actual peels across the sky. The light was always there...yes, that's right. It was always there but I couldn't see it because the angle of the Earth to the Sun kept it unrevealed. Jesus Christ is with us constantly – He's always here in our heart...but the angle of our hearts must be right for Him to be revealed.

We don't know that day/time exactly, like we can project the dawn, because we don't have all the data, but we do have the signs. A woman doesn't know the moment of birth until it happens. She knows a probable time frame and she knows the signs of anticipation, but the moment is left hidden even in a C-section where there is surgical intervention. That moment of birth is a revealing of the hidden anticipation of something long awaited. Jesus is coming. The signs of the times are appearing everywhere. Like the song says, "I can almost hear that first sound of the trumpet as Gabriel sounds the call" ...all of Earth in breathless anticipation...and yet...wait...I forgot my bag! My people!...isn't it time you made telling others a priority? Isn't it time you begin to chirp that the dawn is breaking? Do you feel it? The midnight cry is almost upon us..."when Jesus steps out on a cloud to call His children...."

My question: What are God-worshipers like?
Your answer: Arrows aimed at God's bull's-eye.
They settle down in a promising place; Their kids inherit a prosperous farm. God-friendship is for God-worshipers; They are the ones He confides in. If I keep my eyes on God, I won't trip over my own feet
Psalms 25:12-15

God's Arrows!

If you notice, this picture isn't straight on; that's because it is shot from the aim of the viewer. It is a gorgeous photo of a field of cotton growing in a field. I like to think it is a prosperous farm that a family will pass down through the generations. This is the field of promise God wants us to find. He wants us to be worshippers that settle down in a promising place of confidential trust in who He is, keeping our eyes on Him. Oh, it is so easy to wander off, chasing after the latest and greatest of things that lead us through fields of wonder, but how spectacular it is to stay on target. God's target – the bull's eye – is the sublime place of worship. How do we aim to be successful in life? By aiming at God's center of worship. My boys loved bow hunting for a brief sojourn of life. We converted the attic into a target range, took membership at a bow hunting club, had the best in equipment of bows/arrows, and even got targets to set up in the yard shaped like deer and bears.

The ultimate test was the bear hunting trip to Canada. They spent hours aiming at the target and practicing to be ready. The day arrived and the anticipation was there, gear packed and loaded, all prepared in our minds. Then upon arrival, the trajectory changed! The aim wasn't from the ground, straight across, because shooting an arrow at a live bear that way was dangerous – duh!!! Why didn't we think of that and practice that way? The target and trajectory had changed. Now they had to shoot from up in a stand and down towards the target.

The guides gave direction and instructions. My youngest decided he'd use a gun rather than a bow because it was more accurate and he had used a gun from a tree stand while hunting – he was the only one who got a bear. The others shot and wounded, but didn't get the kill shot because their arrow didn't hit the mark due to lack of experience in that trajectory/situation. When we as worshippers of God practice in a field of self-indulgence, then our aim at God's target is off and we miss the mark as we set our eyes on things of earth that fail rather than the things of God. When we aim towards God and put our whole trust in Him and our focus on Him practicing to be what He desires as we worship only Him, then our aim is true and our arrows find the mark. David asks what a worshipper of God is like? The answer is they are friends of God-close confidantes who hear His voice and know His aim. They keep their eyes on Him instead of tripping themselves up by looking around them at others. They settle in Him and pass that Faith-walk of God's promises down through the generations because their aim is true as they practice it daily, hourly… constantly. I think of all the people I know whom I call upon for extreme prayer needs.

What is the common denominator? I know God hears them because I see evidence of his goodness in their lives and I see the complete peace of serenity through the storms of life. The "yea, though I walk through the shadow of death, I will fear no evil" kind of peace. That only comes through practice. That only comes from aiming at God's bull's eye and getting accurate from constant automation of aim. Where is your aim? Are you practicing at the wrong target or trajectory? Begin to put yourselves in His field, aiming towards His desires, and watch your accuracy increase and your confidence build. Begin to worship the Creator just for who He is and not what He does. Watch and see. Practice makes perfect!

We look at this Son and see the God who cannot be seen. We look at this Son and see God's original purpose in everything created. For everything, absolutely everything, above and below, visible and invisible, rank after rank after rank of angels everything got started in Him and finds its purpose in Him. He was there before any of it came into existence and holds it all together right up to this moment. And when it comes to the church, He organizes and holds it together, like a head does a body. He was supreme in the beginning and leading the resurrection parade-He is supreme in the end. From beginning to end He's there, towering far above everything, everyone. So spacious is He, so expansive, that everything of God finds its proper place in Him without crowding. Not only that, but all the broken and dislocated pieces of the universe people and things, animals and atoms--get properly fixed and fit together in vibrant harmonies, all because of His death, His blood that poured down from the cross.

Colossians 1:15-20

Purposed!

What is my purpose? Who am I? Where do I belong in the vastness of life? Why am I alive? These are questions that plague every single soul on earth – until they find Him. It is the intangible we search for in our hearts and minds. It is the reason so many wind up in bad situations and thousands of self-help books are created about it. One of my son's favorite books as a child is called "The Giving Tree". It is a book about the sacrifices the tree made in achieving purpose to a person. From the moment we are born, we seek to be a part of His divine plan because we are seeking our place in Him. The world offers so many other things to us: from money to entertainment, drugs and fame, shame and reproach, highs and lows; but in all of them, once achieved, there is nothing but emptiness; unless it is purposed through Him. I look at the people in scriptures and see the stories of their life unfold much like I see the stories of today unfold on Facebook.

They have ups and downs, pressures and promises, wins and losses, highs and lows; each striving and straining towards attaining their purpose. When we find our place in Him we are placed in perfect harmony with the things around us and the rest of life is only a part of the beautiful music that He's making, instead of strident chords of discontent. Life isn't perfect. Life isn't fair. Money may make things easier, but it creates its own set of problems. Love isn't without its own issues, either; except God's love, which is perfect. We as a people will never be happy until we find our purpose in Him. We will continue to strive and fuss in our uncomfortable situations, moving from place to place in our minds and hearts, as well as our physical being, until we achieve the discovery of ourselves in Him. So how is that done? By going after Him with all of your being. I know that sounds too easy and too good to be true but when you pursue God with all of you, He picks up all the pieces of your brokenness and makes a beautiful masterpiece of stained glass that hangs in His gallery of purpose. He fits you into the harmony of life, playing your part to the melody that He wrote. There is an old song I love called "In My Heart There Rings a Melody of Love." It is a classic song – beautiful lyrics that illustrate this verse of scripture so well.

Everything in nature craves to be a part of His eternal song – you can hear it…if you listen. There are phone apps that have recordings of plants singing to the rhythms of the earth. Everything is purposed to worship our Creator. Begin your day in worship. Worship in the good and in the bad. Hold on to your song as you find your purpose in Him, for it's already there…in you. This purposeful melody is waiting to be sung to Him. Seek your purpose by worshipping Him and the rest will align. There will still be ups/downs, but you'll have joy in all of them. Seek Him and He will put the rest together in perfect harmony!

Then I observed all the work and ambition motivated by envy. What a waste! Smoke. And spitting into the wind. One handful of peaceful repose Is better than two fistfuls of worried work- More spitting into the wind. It's better to have a partner than go it alone. Share the work, share the wealth. And if one falls down, the other helps,
But if there's no one to help, tough! Two in a bed warm each other. Alone, you shiver all night.
By yourself you're unprotected.
With a friend you can face the worst. Can you round up a third? A three stranded rope isn't easily snapped
Ecclesiastes
4:4, 6, 9-12

Spitting into the Wind!

I can honestly say that I have never spit into the wind, but I know what happens when you do; I have tried tossing my gum out my car window once when I was little - it wasn't a good idea. Solomon spends time instructing about wisdom from God against envy and greed because he sees what it does. He sees the trials that it causes, the stress and the strife. He sees the challenges in a life based on always trying to get ahead and never being content with where God has you. I love the camaraderie at my office. The sense that we are all pulling together as one towards a goal makes us stand together - for each other - like nothing else. I watch as one trainer sends a need out and the others step up to meet that need via text. This mindset is what God wants for His children. He wants us to realize that when we all pull together in His direction, we move closer more quickly, and with strength.

I once watched a television show about the Dust Bowl and blizzards on the plains, where a rope tied from building to building; this became a way of getting from place to place safely because vision was lost during the blinding snow or dust, as eyes had to be closed and heads covered. When Solomon shares here in the value of a three stranded rope, I get it. Each strand woven together and held by God's hand allows us to walk through tough storms knowing He is there because we feel His strand in our hands even while we are climbing, or clinging, to that rope in the midst of a storm. We can securely close our eyes to the things that seem to overwhelm us and trust that He is holding that rope secure to the place He is taking us. When we bind with others on that same journey, we are strengthening each other - as we journey together. It's not easy, but it can still be joyous and full of laughter if we will relax in Him, knowing that He has us.

When we allow fear, doubt, and worry to blind us - along with envy, unfulfilled wishes and dreams - we cut at the rope that is securely fastening us. When we bemoan and get fraught with all the things not happening in our time and our way, we are letting go of His rope that guides us and then opening our eyes to the cutting winds, dirt, smoke; and then spitting into that same wind. When you spit into the wind, it comes back all over you in a nasty spray. Better to swallow that spittle of pride and keep holding onto the rope of God that guides you safely than to let go and spit the nastiness of life at those around you, for then you only end up covered in regrets and muck. When life seems to be bringing you little, tuck in tighter to who He is and He will guide you. His arms will hold you and He will be your strength.

Jesus Said. "Go ahead
get out of here!" crazed the pig's
stampeded over cliff into the sea and
drowned. Scared to death the swineherds
bolted. They told everyone back in town what
had happened to the madmen and the pigs.
Those who heard about it were angry about
the drowned pigs.
A mob formed and demanded that Jesus get
out and not come back.
Matthew 8:32-34

Grip of Fear!

The first occurrence of swine sickness wasn't exactly like the swine flu we have today, but it has similarities – mainly fear! In this account, Jesus and His disciples have just ministered to a group of people, gotten into a boat and crossed the sea to a new place. The disciples had just seen Jesus command the winds and waves to cease; they were still stunned and in awe as they came to the beach cliffs. There they encountered two men who had terrified the village so long that no one felt safe walking that way. They were full of demons, who immediately recognized Jesus. Yes, the winds and waves recognized Him and His authority, and the demons of hell recognized Him and His authority, but see what happens...

The people of the village have lived In terror for years and these demons ask to go into the swine. The pigs, unlike the people, ran off the cliff rather than live in terror. The herders watching them freaked out and went into town, bringing back a group of people who were rude and unaccepting. Instead of recognizing the authority that He had and receiving Him, the rebuffed Him and angrily asked Him to leave. How many times has God moved for us, doing things in our lives to improve our situation, relieving our lives of fear, ignorance and evil, but we fail to acknowledge His authority and then reject Him because it affected our pocketbook, or our plans? I think of children who don't understand something and while you are helping them, they pitch a royal fit because they aren't getting their way. How guilty we are of missing out on the blessings of God because we are sick with the disease of "ME". He came to deliver, but His deliverance brought consequences which angered the people, so they refused His healing. They had their worth wrapped up in the pigs. They had let fear dominate and have control for so long that anger flared up and took over, robbing them of their blessings. Just imagine if they had surrendered all, thanking Jesus for delivering those two men? How many people could have had their lives changed through healing and salvation? Grip of fear and resulting anger rules in many lives. It is a very real disease that torments our culture. Fear and anger coexist, each adding to the emotional response of the other but just like the winds and waves recognized His voice, so do the emotional responses and spirits that dwell among us. Speak to the fear, depression and anger in Jesus' authority. Sickness cannot stay, fear cannot stay, anger cannot stay...all must go in the name of Jesus! You can walk in His authority or you can be there on the sidelines, watching in awe as His authority reigns. His dominion doesn't change just because you ask Him to leave so you can dwell in your pit of fear/anger. The only thing that changes is the potential to be free. Jesus has all authority under heaven and in all the Earth but He is a gentleman.

He will not force His way Into your life for salvation. He offers it as a gift of life that you must choose. The demons in the men recognized that. They asked to go into the swine and then drowned the swine because they knew and recognized Jesus' authority. The swine flu is very real but the "swine flu" we are discussing here is too and each of these can be deadly. One may hurt the body while the other can kill the soul. Jesus' authority extends to both. He is not limited by man's expectations nor his finiteness. His authority is absolute and He has given us His authority to walk in...so why are we not commanding the mountains in our lives to move, casting out the demons of fear and anger and all the others, leading the way to Jesus? Isn't it time to begin walking in His authority?

So let's not allow ourselves to get fatigued doing good. At the right time we will harvest a good crop if we don't give up, or quit. Right now, therefore, every time we get the chance, let us work for the benefit of all, starting with the people closest to us in the community of faith. For my part, I am going to boast about nothing but the Cross of our Master, Jesus Christ. Because of that Cross, I have been crucified in relation to the world, set free from the stifling atmosphere of pleasing others and fitting into the little patterns that they dictate. Can't you see the central issue in all this? It is not what you and I do-submit to circumcision, reject circumcision. It is what God is doing, and He is creating something totally new, a free life! All who walk by this standard are the true Israel of God- His chosen people. Peace and mercy on them!
Galatians 6:9-10, 14-16

The Doing!

The days were long and arduous as I pushed through, working despite the pain. I kept pouring and pouring out of myself, growing more and more fatigued as I failed to fill up as often as I needed until suddenly, I was on empty. I had no more to give, I thought. I was spent. I went home depleted and exhausted with nothing left over for the ones who needed me the most. You see, I had given of myself without refilling until I hit that breaking point. So I went to Jesus and begin to refill. But why did I wait? The Living Water is like a waterfall that constantly flows. It is our choice to be under the flow – He is always there and He is constant. Peace, mercy and freedom all come because of the cross and in that filling and refilling we can enjoy the refreshing. We don't ever have to wait.

I love mint tea because it is so refreshing and light. I always keep a gallon or two at my house and as soon as I see I am running low, I get ready to brew a gallon from my ground mint supply. When my ground mint is low, I go to the source, pick the leaves, roast them and then I can brew a new gallon. But it takes time to do all that. One, because I have to keep that mint healthy and growing so I have a supply source. The reason I share this is to illustrate that sometimes it takes work tending the garden of your mind and heart; to keep it fertile and growing so that you're ready to receive and give. There's no point to pouring water into an empty field that has no crop, as it will just become a muddy mess. In order to drink from The Source and fill to overflowing so you can give, you must first cultivate the fruit. It takes work to grow. You must put in the effort and you must stay refreshed in the doing so that you do not grow stagnant and unfruitful. As wrote to the Paul Galatians here, he usually used a scribe, but he wrote these words from his own hand, under the anointing. It isn't about us or what we do. It is about what God is doing.

As I drove home from the airport yesterday, I saw a young man laboring under a heavy load as he walked down the road. God spoke to me and said his load is too heavy. Pick him up and share my life with Him. This is something I just don't do in today's world but God told me to do it. So I stopped my car, rolled down the window and asked if he'd like a ride. As he got in, I handed him a bottle of water and began to share God's love. He started crying and said that he really needed to hear that, he said he was raised in church but had been in a bad place because he had been angry that God had allowed ugly things to happen to him. We arrived at his home and his girlfriend came out. We talked briefly of God's love and both prayed with me for God's saving grace to be renewed in their lives. I was tired as I drove home from a full week of doing, but God was constantly flowing through me and in His time; I was a tributary of His grace.

You see, we have a choice. I could've chosen not to pick that young man up and I would've still been tired but I would've missed out on the opportunity of blessing from that moment – that glimpse of Heaven. Your life is free. Your choices are yours by the grace of God. He is creating this new thing in you. You can choose to work the ground and receive His blessings or to labor in exhaustion and miss out. The choice is yours – working, but full; or tired and empty.

The revelation of God is whole and pulls our lives together. The sign-posts of God are clear and point out the right road. The life-maps of God are right, showing the way to joy. The directions of God are plain and easy on the eyes God's reputation is twenty four -carat gold, with a lifetime guarantee. The decisions of God are accurate down to the nth degree.
Psalms 19:7-9

Golden Reputation!

A sterling character is considered to be the highest compliment as it indicates an untarnished silver which is very valuable. Here, David says God's reputation is that of gold. I couldn't help but think of this beautiful photo my friend Uriah posted yesterday of God's handiwork. God has the eye of an artist and has given Uriah that talent also. Uriah took this photo on a nature walk. You can clearly see the road and I picture it with the signposts of God saying yes, there are shadows of life that hang over you but I am leading you to a place of wonder and golden opportunity if you will lean into me. That glimpse of golden joy on this life-map shows God's 24-carat gold reputation. You see, the higher the golden content, the heavier and weightier the gold is, which adds to its value, but the thing with gold is that the higher the carat, the more malleable the gold. God's reputation doesn't depend on you and me, but He stretches His golden reputation of joy and love out over us as a covering. He gives us His revelation to pull our lives together as a whole.

His directions are as plain and easy on the eye as this gorgeous photo. His decisions are as accurate as the artist's aim in this photo down to the Nth degree. You see, a photo has to have the right composition and right timing and right lighting and so many other right things to come together in this stunning manner. God's directs our lives just like this. He pulls us together down the right road with clear directions, giving us the stunning viewpoint, right aim, composition and lighting for our lives to be a Masterpiece of His choosing and His design. You are God's masterpiece, just as this photo is a stunning revelation of God's glory. You gave a lifetime guarantee that He will be with you to guide you and direct you down all the paths of life into the stunning golden opportunity of joy through His loving grace, if you will but trust Him. A golden reputation is much better than a sterling one because gold doesn't tarnish, grow old, lose value, nor degrade. They say a picture is worth a thousand words so I think these 70 or so words of God via a king with this stunning picture is worth a million or more! Golden!

At that time, this song will be sung in the country of Judah: We have a strong city, Salvation City, built and fortified with salvation. Throw wide the gates so good and true people can enter. People with their minds set on you, you keep completely whole, Steady on their feet, because they keep at it and don't quit. Depend on God and keep at it because in the Lord God you have a sure thing. Those who lived high and mighty He knocked off their high horse. He used the city built on the hill as fill for the marshes.All the exploited and outcast peoples build their lives
on the reclaimed land.
Isaiah 26:1-6

The Sure Thing!

If there's one thing that I know is that things will change. Nothing ever stays the same, except God. The promises of men – politicians and others – will always fail, but God's love doesn't fail. I love how this verse starts...at this time.... this song will be sung.....we have a strong city of Salvation. A city is founded on principles and strong connection to the center of purpose. Salvation is the surety. Salvation is the bedrock. Salvation is the anchor. Jesus is the Rock of our salvation. The strong city that is built is built on Him. He threw wide the gates opening them so that good and true people can enter through His sacrifice! Each one who enters here comes in confidence because their mind is fixated on Him.

What fractures a mirror or window is a crack that starts as a simple chip. When the mind starts with a simple toehold of doubt/fear, it grows or runs into a crack of disbelief which easily fractures the confidence in God. Salvation is the city of safety. When you depend on God and stay confident in His goodness without quitting, you walk through the open gates of surety. Recently I watched some workers take a hill in our area and tear it down to fill low areas and flatten it into a place to build. This is the path that Jesus is and has created. He has torn down the hill of self-righteousness and self-reliance by evening the field to those who truly depend on Him. When your eyes are on Him and not on what will happen based on circumstances, you allow the miracles to happen. Jesus doesn't depend on man to make things happen.

God doesn't need men to be God. God is God and depending on Him requires us to get our eyes off situations and people. Seating your mind on God and remaining steady in confidence in Him despite what you see takes a constancy. Every time the tiny pebbles of life hit against the windshield of your walk you must reset so that no cracks form. The seating of confidence is in Salvation. Salvation is the founding principle of the city of life and the place of celebration. No matter what changes occur in your life, fix your mind on Him – the author and finisher of our Faith! Do not let anything steal your foundation. Celebrate at this time! Sing a song of Salvation! God isn't done! God isn't weak! God isn't without! God is able! God is willing! God is good! God is the Sure Thing when all else fails!

Everything in the world is about to be wrapped up, so take nothing for granted. Stay wide-awake in prayer. Most of all, love each other as if your life depended on it. Love makes up for practically anything. Be quick to give a meal to the hungry, a bed to the homeless—cheerfully. Be generous with the different things God gave you, passing them around so all get in on it: if words, let it be God's words; if help, let it be God's hearty help. That way, God's bright presence will be evident in everything through Jesus, and He'll get all the credit as the One mighty in everything—encores to the end of time. Oh, yes!

1 Peter
4:7 - 11

Wide Awake!

It is the middle of the night and I am wide awake praying. Most of you will read this long after it is written, but God showed me a vision of His desires for us as I sit here on my couch in the dead of night. This picture is the night sky-the moon reflection looks like a white horse coming through the clouds. This is how suddenly Jesus will appear! Even now, signs of the times are appearing everywhere. Peter saw the end times approaching hundreds of years ago and wrote that we should take nothing for granted, but to stay wide awake in prayer. What is the difference in being wide awake and just awakened?

When you are awake, it is the opposite of sleeping, which can be translated as being alive. Wide awake is fully and energetically alive in prayer. Many of us have not disciplined nor trained ourselves in prayer so we, like the disciples, tire easily and either give out …or go to sleep. Jesus knew this of us and that's why He asked those closest to Him to go and pray with Him in the Garden of Gethsemane. He knew that we are easily lulled asleep by the quiet of the night. We get a false sense of security when things are unshaken and undisrupted. Our bodies haven't been trained to be alert in prayer but rather lulled into a false sense of security in night. Night is the most dangerous time for prey because it is the time where their senses are dulled because they cannot see everything clearly. We are the prey, as the devil goes about in the dark seeking whom he may devour. We are being lulled into a false pretense that all is well and we can slumber rather than stay wide awake and tuned up in prayer. My husband has a deer camera in the area where he hunts and he shows me pictures of the animals that come into his hunting area at night seeking food. The first time the camera flashes and makes a noise, they appear startled but when they are un-harmed, they begin to mistrust that still, small sense within them that all isn't as it should be.

They begin to yum-it-up on the feed and ignore the warning signs which could ultimately lead to their demise. We too are often tricked because we are fed well in America with freedoms and constant availability of the gospel in varies forms - from Bibles all over our houses to online access of church services. We spend less and less time in prayer and watchful anticipation, as we feel the dregs of sleep pulling on our beings. Jesus is coming! Are you wide awake in prayer, loving others into His kingdom? Are you joyously generous with God's Providence that He has allowed you to steward? Do the people around you see God in your actions, hear Him in your words and feel Him in your love and deeds? Wide awake? Begin to pray. Pray for our country. Pray for God's hand to move in lives. As the night calls, can you stay awake in Him and pray? Have you disciplined yourself to listen for His voice alone and not the call of the flesh? Be alert! Be ready! Stay awake! Wide awake in His presence is the place of safety in these end times.

I bless God every chance I get; my lungs expand with His praise. I live and breathe God; if things aren't going well, hear this and be happy: Join me in spreading the news; together let's get the word out. God met me more than halfway, He freed me from my anxious fears. Look at Him; give Him your warmest smile. Never hide your feelings from Him. When I was desperate, I called out, and God got me out of a tight spot.
Psalms 34:1-6

Look at Him!

When doing brain training, it is important to add mental load and distractions because these are things we deal with daily in our lives. If things are more difficult, then they can get the load of distractions removed...and they become easier. Look at the arrow in the picture as it points a certain direction. The direction it is pointing becomes the direction in which your eyes travel. Try to read the words while looking at the arrow and you'll find it is much harder to read left to right because the arrow has your brain wanting to read right to left. The purpose is that you train yourself to ignore the distractions.

God meets us more than halfway, but we must focus on Him rather than life's distractions or we make our situation much harder. If we begin to focus on Him and only Him, then the path of life becomes easier and we train ourselves to overcome obstacles, distractions, and temptations by looking towards Him and not towards that which leads us off path. God hears you. He hears you and wants you to join in spreading the good news and be freed from your anxious fears. Never try to hide from Him. Every time I call to Him, He hears me. The issue is that I must remember to call to Him. Spiritually, He's right there as I walk on the water beside Him, focusing on Him, but when I get distracted by the storms and waves around me, my focus shifts … and I begin to sink. If I call to Him, He lifts me back to Him, but if in my stubbornness I insist on going on my own, the water becomes deeper and harder to manage as I try to swim alone.

I begin to tire and fatigue. I become desperate, then holler out to Him. He lifts me back to the place of safety. I see my own children trying things on their own when I know they need help - even now - and I watch them struggle, knowing that I can help, want to help, desire to help, but they are young adults now and must ask...I remember this from when they were toddlers - the No, me stage. I wanna do it myself is a fleshly mindset. It is selfish and inward viewing rather than being open to God's perspective. Look at Him! Switch your viewpoint. Begin to praise God and bless Him rather than bemoan your circumstances. Begin to breathe Him in and live in Him. When things are going bad, look at Him and give Him your warmest smile, filled with confidence in who He is, for this is the time He will show out the most!

Lord, see my smile. Feel my heartbeat as I look to you! I will not be distracted by the things around me but I will focus on you and bless you with every breath. Help me God! Pull me back up from my own mess. Set me up to walking on the waters of life with you by my side.

Everything that goes into a life of pleasing God has been miraculously given to us by getting to know, personally and intimately, the One who invited us to God.
The best invitation we ever received!
We were also given absolutely terrific promises to pass on to you--your tickets to participation in the life of God after you turned your back on a world corrupted by lust.

So don't lose a minute in building on what you've been given, complementing your basic faith with good character, spiritual understanding, alert discipline, passionate patience, reverent wonder, warm friendliness, and generous love, each dimension fitting into and developing the others. With these qualities active and growing in your lives, no grass will grow under your feet, no day will pass without its reward as you mature in your experience of our Master Jesus. Without these qualities you can't see what's right before you, oblivious that your old sinful life has been wiped off the books.
2 Peter 1:3-9

Dimensions!

A friend from church posted a series of pictures which resulted in the final piece of art that had taken her 4 weeks of diligence to make. She has painstakingly drawn and colored carefully to match a photo of what God created with a breath and a word. It took a precious amount of time and effort as she diligently drew and colored each feather, building the dimensions upon one another so that the colors blended seamlessly and beautifully. Everything that goes into the life of pleasing God has been miraculously given to us by getting to know Jesus personally and intimately. The promises of God have amazing potential in our lives, but, just like a ticket to a wonderful vacation, we must accept it first; then we must build on it. A person doesn't just decide to go on vacation and leave. It's a process of planning and working out those details.

You have been given all the tools needed to build the life God desires for you, but you must act. The qualities listed by Peter here are those that you must build into dimensions of your life. Without these, you cannot have the full vision. You see through the glass darkly...but as the Light builds into your life, you painstakingly build the dimensions of God's vision in your life.

Good character takes time and effort, which in turn builds spiritual understanding that comes from the discipline of an alert reading of The Word, praying with passion, patient waiting to see what miracles God will reveal in reverent wonder, approaching each person and opportunity with warm friendliness and generous love. You see, these are all the dimensions of His glory that build together to form an amazing viewpoint of His glory. The two photos here are the same backdrop.... but one has more light, which gives more opportunities to see the masterpiece that God created one morning as a whisper of His love. Without the light, it is hard to see the full beauty of His creation. Without these traits that bring The Light into this darkened world, it is hard to see the truth that God has already done! Your sins have been erased and your life divine has already begun.

Begin to walk in His light by accepting His generous love and divine gift of salvation. Then you will go into the house of God so you can be surrounded by the warm friendliness of His saints and in reverent wonder experience the passionate patience God gives us as we develop in Him; working the alert discipline of the Christ-like walk into our everyday lives so that you can achieve the spiritual understanding that leads to good character. See how that works? God works into you the promises and gifts He has already given, developing you so that you, the Masterpiece, can painstakingly see what He has already miraculously given to you when you turn your back on the world and begin to see Him for who He truly is.

Learn to appreciate and give dignity to your body, not abusing it, as is so common among those who know nothing of God.
Don't run roughshod over the concerns of your brothers and sisters. Their concerns are God's concerns, and he will take care of them. We've warned you about this before. God hasn't invited us into a disorderly, grungy life but into something holy and beautiful-as beautiful on the inside as the outside.
1 Thessalonians 4:4-7

Ditch the Grunge!

Dignity is a tough word to define in today's society, as many have thwarted its meaning. Being worthy of honor or glory defines the way we are to treat our bodies: as a holy temple where the Most High dwells. We are told to learn to appreciate and give dignity by not abusing our bodies as those who know nothing of God.

I'll admit this has been a tough one for me, because I wasn't born with a perfect specimen in my eyes. As a young person, my body was not up to the Barbie standard, so I got a lot of put downs and mistreatment from many in school, church and home life. I was made fun of and mocked with silly songs, harsh words, critiques, and criticisms by many resulting in a yo-yo dietary habit that led to intense physical exercise abusing my body. I had trauma to my body in the form of emergency surgical procedures and this only added to my dilemma but then...God. One day, I'll never forget it, as it was the day of mindset change. The day God became so very real to me. I had been saved and baptized both in water by age 7 and the Holy Spirit at age 11, so I had a confidence in God, but on this day in 1990-I realized that God had confidence in me and it changed my perspective. I was walking across campus at my college and I heard a child call to me by name so I turned. That was unusual but even more, she told her mom, "Look at her, she's the most beautiful person I have ever seen; she glows from inside." Of course, I thanked her and then went about my business.

I didn't realize that a holy moment had occurred and changed me until the next morning as I looked into the mirror. Then I realized that was God speaking through the child. As I looked into the mirror, I saw something holy and beautiful on the inside and the outside. I begin to realize that no matter what this body is in man's eyes, it is a vessel filled with His purpose. My hands, feet and abilities are here to serve the concerns of my fellow believers and to be God's hands and feet into this world. I have never even told my husband this, but that is actually how I knew he was my intended spouse. Wes told me that he thought I was the most beautiful person he had ever seen with an internal glow about me and up to that point, he was the only person other than the child who had ever told me that in that holy way. That glow is love.: the filling of God's love dispensed into me by my parents demonstrating His love. It is said that Beauty is in the eye of the Beholder because we each have unique opinions of beauty. I'm not going to say that I was never told I was pretty by my parents, but we easily dismiss that knowing that they are biased. I constantly compared my body to others until that holy moment. It was a beginning of the learning to appreciate and give dignity to the vessel that God gave me to live in. I haven't ever abused any substances nor put any alcohol, tobacco, etc. into my body to harm it, but I still have had health issues. My body isn't perfect but it is yielded. It is a vessel of Christ the King. I'm not a disorderly, grungy mess because I see myself as a temple or place of Holiness unto Him. This is a learning process. Begin by treating your body as a holy place where A King resides or A Queen if easier for you to picture. Your concerns are God's concerns. Hear Him telling you that you are beautiful and wonderful to Him and begin to praise Him. Allow His light to gather strength and light you from the inside to the outside for that is the definition of true beauty that deserves dignity. Ditch the Grunge from the false viewpoint of self and begin to see His beauty in you. You are beautiful and a masterpiece of His making!

"Stay alert. This is hazardous work i'm assigning you.
You re going to be like sheep running through a wolf pack, so don't call attention to yourselves. Be as shrewd as a snake, inoffensive as a dove. "If you don't go all the way with me, through thick and thin, you don't deserve me.
If your first concern is to look after yourself, you'll never find yourself. But if you forget about yourself and look to me, you'll find both yourself and me."
Matthew 10: 16, 38-39

Hazards Ahead!

Lately the road to/from my home has had a lot of construction activity. Not because they are repairing the road, but because of installation of new electrical cell towers. This means that taking care to pay attention to what's happening around you is essential to safety. The workers must really be on alert because with all the technical work and the distractions of drivers, the dangers are very real. Jesus is telling us the same in this passage. He knows as He sends His disciples out, that there are many who will do whatever it takes to destroy the ministry and tear down His kingdom. But it doesn't come from the outside. The true dangers are the wolves in sheep's clothing tearing apart the sheep as if they are protecting the flock. Over and over lately, I have seen so many who are devout and loving people of God being torn apart by those who claim to love God. The love of God is not in you when you are sniping at another child of God. Being stealthy like a snake, but harmless as a dove as we go through trials and temptations is tough. Our natural instinct is to strike back at those who are offensive to us, but Jesus instructs us to instead move as a sheep through a pack of wolves. He wants us to go about His business confident in Him, but wary of those around us who are not running with Him. If a sheep is comfortable with the wolf, perhaps it is not a sheep at all. If those who prefer to socialize in places, ways, and situations that are not the acceptable in the house of God nor uplifting to His glory, perhaps those are not people of God at all. If one calls themselves a Christian, yet refuses to accept ALL of God's word as truth, perhaps they are not truly walking in the light, but rather walking in the shadows.

As I recently walked across a dappled field, I came across uneven terrain. I chose to transverse it even though the steps ahead were unclear. The hidden hazards got my attention as my foot stepped awkwardly into a hidden hole and my ankle twisted. Immediately, I became more cautious and careful of the path: more alert, more tuned into the surroundings and more watchful. These days/times are fraught with tension but if we keep our focus on the eternal and stay the course with Christ as our guide, we will make it gloriously to the end. Stepping off the designated path into the unknown to take a shortcut didn't work out for me. I ended up with a swollen ankle and tender foot for days after I had retreated back to the marked path. Yes, the marked path was rocky and filled bumps, but it had been designed for travel unlike the detour I chose. Hidden dangers and hazards of life abound but we have the choose to stay the course with the Master's guidance towards reward or to detour through the unknown hazards alone. Stay alert. Travel lightly and forget about yourself, keeping your eyes on Him-the author and finisher of our faith.

www.ingramcontent.com/pod-product-compliance
Lightning Source LLC
Chambersburg PA
CBHW042022090426
42811CB00016B/1709